Please ...th

"Each page sings Rempel's commitment to faith transmission through activities, presence, and storytelling."
—*Marlene Harder Bogard, minister of Christian formation, Western District Conference of Mennonite Church USA*

"The discussion questions and the practical suggestions stir the imagination."
—*Laura Loewen, seniors ministry coordinator, Emmanuel Mennonite Church, Abbotsford, British Columbia*

"Elsie Rempel applies her zest, experience, and creativity as she weaves together the gifts and needs of children and seniors. Both generations have a higher calling to be the church together. We recommend this book as an instrument in revitalizing the health of both family and church."
—*Robert J. and Irene Suderman, retired leaders in Mennonite Church Canada*

"Christian faith needs to be shared in creative, loving, and challenging ways with each new generation. I encourage the older generation (and the younger ones, too) to read, discuss, and enact Elsie Rempel's thought-provoking book."
—*Larry Kehler, retired pastor, journalist, and administrator with Mennonite Church Canada and Mennonite Central Committee*

"Understanding each phase of a grandchild's development can go a long way toward knowing how to encourage them on their faith journey. I highly recommend this book as a helpful study for senior groups."
—*Marian Wiens, retired marriage and family therapist, mission worker with the Korea Anabaptist Center*

Please Pass the Faith
The Art of Spiritual Grandparenting

by Elsie H. R. Rempel

Herald Press
Waterloo, Ontario
Harrisonburg, Virginia

Library and Archives Canada Cataloguing in Publication
Rempel, Elsie H. R., 1952-
    Please pass the faith : the art of spiritual grandparenting /
by Elsie H.R. Rempel.
ISBN 978-0-8361-9642-9
    1. Grandparenting—Religious aspects—Christianity. 2.
Grandparent and child—Religious aspects—Christianity. 3.
Children and older people—Religious aspects—Christianity. 4.
Mentoring—Religious aspects—Christianity. I. Title.

BV4580.R44 2012   248.8'5   C2012-902802-9

Unless otherwise noted, Scripture text is quoted, with per-
mission, from the *New Revised Standard Version,* © 1989,
Division of Christian Education of the National Council of
Churches of Christ in the United States of America.

PLEASE PASS THE FAITH: THE ART OF SPIRITUAL
GRANDPARENTING
Copyright © 2012 by Herald Press, Harrisonburg, Virginia 22802
        Released simultaneously in Canada by Herald Press,
        Waterloo, Ontario N2L 6H7. All rights reserved.
Canadiana Entry Number: C2012-902802-9
Library of Congress Control Number: 2012938090
International Standard Book Number: 978-0-8361-9642-9
Printed in United States of America
Cover design and background photo by Merrill Miller
Cover photo by Patricia Casanave/iStockphoto/Thinkstock

16 15 14 13 12   10 9 8 7 6 5 4 3 2 1

To order or request information, please call 1-800-245-7894 in
the U.S. or 1-800-631-6535 in Canada.
Or visit www.heraldpress.com.

To God's children, of all ages, who connect across generational divides.

Table of Contents

Preface and Acknowledgements

The seeds for *Please Pass the Faith: The Art of Spiritual Grandparenting* were gleaned from the findings of a Canada-wide listening tour in 2005 by Robert J. Suderman, who was then General Secretary of Mennonite Church Canada. During that tour, he visited each of the denomination's 225 congregations to gain an understanding of church gifts, needs, wants, and concerns.

A broadly identified need emerged for the development of resources aimed at ministry with younger seniors, the rapidly growing group of newly retired people known as "the boomers." This bulge of seniors also needed to learn how to affirm and bless younger people in the church family.

Since I had lots of experience with children's ministry, and as a grandmother had begun to learn about life in senior land, the task for developing resources was passed on to me. So I began. And I kept learning from my children and grandchildren as I partnered with my husband, their wonderful father and *Opa*—grandfather, in the delightful journey of grandparenting.

Because I am still a healthy sixty-year-old, much of the material about seniors in this book depends more heavily on research than experience. I am not yet old enough to speak with personal authority on something that still lies ahead on my faith journey, and when I get there, I may not have the energy to write about it. When a senior approaches me and says, "So, I hear you've become our expert on aging," I cringe. My humble response is that I am simply trying to learn about aging so that the church can have productive discussions about it. And I invite his or her help.

That has led to some wonderful conversations. I've learned a lot. The life experience and continued leadership of the seniors I have spoken with has been validated. Recognizing the idea that leaders come in all ages and affirming older seniors in the gifts they are still called to share is a counter-cultural message that is deeply welcomed.

This book began to take shape as I experienced grandparenthood, read and observed, talked with other grandparents, wrote, and presented seminars—including some about the art of spiritual grandparenting. In the process, I met Dave Csinos, a fine young practical theologian with a passion for children in the church. At the time, Dave was writing a book on children's ministry[1] and working on his doctor of theology in practical theology. He agreed to read through my first very rough manuscript and helped me update the information about faith formation theory. He also provided me with a great story about his grandmother that you can

---

1. David M. Csinos, *Children's Ministry that Fits: Beyond One-Size-Fits-All Approaches to Nurturing Children's Spirituality* (Eugene: Wipf and Stock, 2011).

read in Chapter Five, and he encouraged me on my venture into book publishing.

Peter Rempel, my dear husband; Dave Bergen, my supervisor at Mennonite Church Canada; Marlene Bogard, my faith formation colleague from Kansas; and Ingrid Schultz, a mature, single pastor with a passion for the younger people of God's family; also read and responded to early drafts. They each provided important guidance from their perspectives.

And then the relationship with my publishers began. Without their skilled eyes, excellent coaching, and editing, this would be a much rougher product. Many thanks to them for their work. I would especially like to thank my editors, Byron Rempel-Burkholder and Amy Gingerich. Thanks also to my friend and colleague, Deborah Froese, who skillfully tackled uncompleted revisions while I was off on a service leave in Zambia. Then she served as my copy editor, cleaning up my writing, making it easier to read and understand. Together we have developed this resource to help young seniors think about their faith forming roles in God's church.

My deepest thanks go to my family for their accompaniment and support on this journey. Without our four grandchildren and their willingness to let me share from our growing treasure trove of memories, this would be a poorer book.

To God be the glory.

Introduction

Who and what are grandparents? Biologically, they are the parents of young people's parents. Sociologically, at least in many traditional cultures, they are the elders, those older people who are revered as the keepers of wisdom. They are often entrusted with major childcare responsibilities, and that gives them a unique opportunity to influence and guide their young charges.

In North America's current youth-glorifying culture, grandparents are sometimes viewed as those who have been left behind, who can't keep up with change. It is common for North American grandparents and grandchildren to live with geographic distance between them. Many of them make the best of exciting and exhausting periodic visits and electronic connections such as emails, social networks, and video chat tools.

For Christians, however, family is more than biological. Jesus redefined family as those who seek and do God's will (Mark 3:34-35). In his last actions on the cross, he created a brand new configuration of family when he named John as the son for his mother, Mary (John 19:26-27). The cross brings the family of Jesus and the disciples of Jesus together, forging a new kind of family. In the book of Acts we read that Jesus' siblings and mother have all claimed a place in the early church, in this reconfigured family of God. Claiming our place in the family of God today opens untapped potential for young people and older people to find each other as spiritual grandparents and grandchildren.

As we seek new and faithful ways of being the church, and to satisfy our needs for relationships across generations, our congregations build family connections through various activities. Intergenerational game nights, storytelling events, and service projects help us get to know and bless each other. In one congregation, a senior woman wanted to help the youth pastor so he asked her to become a prayer ally for one of the congregation's youth. This commitment grew into a ministry across generations. Youth compiled autobiographies with pictures and gave them to seniors who wished to become their friends and prayer supporters. In another congregation, several sets of grandparents whose children and grandchildren live far away made connections with young families who don't have local grandparents. They now relate to each other much like biological families. When my grandchildren moved away for a year, I responded to my own "empty lap syndrome" by teaching a preschool Sunday school class.

God wants us to be in healthy, affectionate relationships with people across the generational spread so that we can be blessed by the unique experiences and perspectives of each age group. Our congregations are a great place to foster such relationships. As we do so, we align with God's intentions for the church and the relational health of God's family is nurtured.

Sometimes relating to our grandchildren and the church's grandchildren overlaps. An eleven year old urban boy told me that he felt closest to God when he was in church with his grandparents in a rural Saskatchewan village. "There were more old people there and they knew so much about God," he said.

Our world and our churches need more grandparents like that.

This book is for older people who wish to grow into such grandparents, whether they seek to fill that role in the lives of their biological grandchildren or in the lives of other young people in their church community. Younger adults may also find this book useful to gain insight into their children's faith development and into their own role in restoring the home as a domestic church. It could help them anticipate their own grandparenting. They might want to pass it on to an older mentor or relative after adding their comments in the margins.

May these reflections find resonance with people of faith who want to serve in grandparenting roles, and with all those who have a heart for passing on a legacy of faith to younger generations.

1

Finding Our Bearings:
What Grandparenting Means Today

We live in an exciting time, a time impacted by climate change, social change, and religious change. It is characterized by a unique set of hopes and fears, by social upheaval, and unanswered questions. Political systems are in flux, giving rise to hope and instability. This is the age in which we find ourselves as grandparents, great uncles, great aunts, and as older mentors of children and youth.

Phyllis Tickle, the renowned New York religion columnist and author of *The Great Emergence*[1], is one of a growing group who claim we are in the middle of a social and religious upheaval that is comparable in size to the Protestant Reformation. Living between major eras presents us with great adversity and great opportunity. If grandparents and other elders have blessed us by passing on their faith in winsome and gracious ways, we have roots that will help us to do the same for future generations. However, we need more than the examples of our elders to relate to today's children and youth,

---

1. Phyllis Tickle, *The Great Emergence* (Grand Rapids: Baker Books, 2008).

who face a unique set of challenges. Our approach to grandparenting may be linked to the past, but we must allow it to evolve in response to today's circumstances. It will then take us on an exciting journey into uncharted territory.

Our present age grows increasingly secular and pluralistic. Christianity has not disappeared and it is not going away, but it has lost the social privilege it held in the West for many centuries. For instance, children and youth may not receive the social encouragement to confess Christ and join the church that their parents and grandparents experienced. On the positive side, this means that young people of today who choose to do so are making more deliberate choices than previous generations did. That bodes well for building a church of passionately committed members. On the sobering side, it is increasingly likely that today's children and grandchildren will choose *not* to follow Christ or join Christ's church. As participants in our current cultural milieu, many may consider themselves to be spiritual, but not Christian.

We can counteract this trend in our current culture by deliberately guiding young people on their journey with Christ and the church. Stories, conversations, celebrations, activities, and rituals define and shape who we are. Sharing our experiences in faith forming ways can be a gift to God's larger family, across generations, for biological and church family grandchildren.

Who Are Today's Grandparents?

Just as the young people of today are different than we were at a younger age, as the grandparents of today we have characteristics that distinguish us from any previous generation of grandparents.

Today's grandparents are younger seniors. In addition to living in the midst of contemporary upheaval, today's younger seniors have a number of unique characteristics. We are part of the "boomer generation," a population bulge which began with increased birth rates after World War II and continued until birth control pills appeared in the early sixties. This means that there are more seniors around today than ever before. Because of good health care and a high standard of living, we expect to live longer lives. Boomers are hard for other age groups to ignore; we have had a major impact on society since birth.

As we enter retirement, boomers' sheer numbers continue to dominate many levels of church and society in North America. With such an impact, the health of society, church, and family, depends upon today's seniors aging well.

Many seniors are part of the "club sandwich" generation. With increased life expectancy for older seniors, many of today's grandparents have family responsibilities toward parents at the same time they are caring for children and grandchildren. As we struggle with our place in the middle of the sandwich, some of us also have to deal with the complex relationships that arise when our grandchildren are members of blended families.

The myriad challenges facing families today bless the wider church by making it aware of changing family dynamics. The church can return this blessing by providing support groups that help families thrive. We need to share our experiences with other church members for this to happen.

Seniors know a lot about doubt and faith. Seniors have learned to read the Bible critically. As part of that critical engagement, some of us discontinued inherited spiritual practices such as family devotions, going to adult Sunday school, or attending midweek Bible studies. Some were influenced by the Jesus Seminar, a movement attempting to reconstruct a historical Jesus, while others reacted to theologians like Marcus Borg and John Shelby Spong, who disputed traditional understandings of Jesus' divinity and came up with new ideas.

Doubts about faith are familiar to many young seniors. As we face the challenges of aging and life transitions, doubt and belief often become close companions. While this could seem like a disadvantage to providing spiritual guidance for biological and church-family grandchildren, experiences with doubt also create avenues for conversation and reflection with youth. If we have the courage and humility to return to or start new spiritual practices, we can travel together with younger people on the journey of faith.

Many seniors are in conversation with people of other religions. Interacting with those of other faiths and integrating that experience with Christian convictions allows seniors to express faith in an increasingly secular and pluralistic society. As a result, seniors can be valued conversation partners for youth and younger adults who are claiming Christian faith in an increasingly post-Christian, North American context. Young people may be more likely to listen graciously to a senior's words of encouragement and caution than they are to listen to the wisdom of their parents, whose authority they may be challenging.

Many seniors are comfortable. Boomers have had more opportunity to plan for retirement, and to save and invest profitably toward that goal, than any previous generation. Many of us can claim "Freedom 55" with enough energy and resources to serve different dimensions of God's family.

Thanks to improved health services and other supports, seniors of today expect to enjoy independent living for a longer period of time than previous generations. As Will Rogers is sometimes credited with saying; "One of the many things no one tells you about aging is that it is such a nice change from being young. Being young is beautiful, but being old is comfortable."[2]

The comfortable part of aging well today does not just benefit seniors—it frees seniors to share the blessings of later years with younger members of God's family. Aging can be both a burden and a blessing, but if we embrace it as a gift to ourselves, our families, our churches, and broader society, the burden will be lessened and the blessing increased for all.

The Influence of Grandparents

When Robert J. Suderman visited each of Mennonite Church Canada's congregations in 2005, he was inspired by seniors who related to other people's children and grandchildren with the same patience and love they showed their biological grandchildren. It was one of many ways he saw and described God at work in our midst in his book, *God's People*

---

2. These lines were originally found as an unattributed quote on Ralph Milton's *Rumours* e-zine, which he stopped producing in early 2011 (http://www.ralphmiltonsrumors.blogspot.com), but a web search suggests that the words belong to Will Rogers (http://www.etni.org.il/farside/willrogers.htm).

Now![3] However, he noticed that such affirmation and love was lacking in many congregations. He wrote, "If seniors have not yet learned how to be proactively affirming, they will need to learn."[4]

Whether we relate to biological grandchildren or to other younger people, learning how to affirm and bless them in proactive ways is critical to their spiritual health and to that of the congregation. This remains so whether or not they choose to become part of the churches with which we identify. It is critical for us to learn to speak freely and appropriately about the spiritual hope that guides our lives.

The bestowing of blessing remains one of the most powerful agents for releasing God's work upon individual lives within both religious and secular contexts. Rachel Naomi Remen's book, *My Grandfather's Blessings*[5], provides a moving testament to the effect of such blessing in a non-religious context. Remen was raised by secular parents but longed for and treasured the weekly Jewish blessing her practicing Jewish grandfather gave her.

Remen's sentiment is just one indicator that grandparents' blessings and testimonies are needed by younger generations, perhaps even more so now than ever before. Boomers have been greatly privileged, and privilege carries responsibility. As the "new" group of young seniors, we are called to use our resources to work with God toward God's reign. This includes fostering intergenerational harmony in our families, church, and society.

---

3. Robert J. Suderman, *God's People Now!* (Waterloo/ Scottdale: Herald Press, 2008).

4. Ibid., 56.

5. Rachel Naomi Remen, MD, *My Grandfather's Blessings* (New York: Riverhead Books, 2000).

The Augsburg Search Institute, George Barna Associates, and other surveyors of social and religious trends have had encouraging findings; parents and grandparents continue to have a significant impact on the attitudes and choices of today's young people. For instance, Christian Smith shares detailed research findings that confirm parents as the single most important influence on the religious lives of young adults. He also claims that the assumption of a sharp religiosity decline during young adult years has been greatly exaggerated.[6]

Recent research on grandparents has focused mainly on the issues and challenges of custodial grandparenting, but as the boomer generation moves into this role, the more typical grandparent-grandchild relationship is receiving some attention.[7]

Unfortunately, the spiritual aspect of this relationship has been neglected in most of those studies. Why? Is it due to the ageism of our youth-glorifying culture? Is it a result of individualism, which tends to separate us from larger social and familial networks? Is it because we live in settings where families are often disconnected from grandparents?

Whatever the reasons for this lack of attention, and whether or not it has been researched and documented, we need to claim and reclaim this significant role. It can also be extended to congregations, where members become family for each other.

---

6. Christian Smith, *Souls in Transition: The Religious & Spiritual Lives of Emerging Adults* (New York: Oxford University Press, 2009).

7. Holly Catterton Allen and Heidi Schultz Oschwald, "God Across the Generations: the Spiritual Influence of Grandparents," in *Nurturing Children's Spirituality: Christian Perspectives and Best Practices*, ed. Holly Catterton Allen (Eugene: Wipf and Stock, 2008), 267–288.

In most traditions, grandparents have been accepted and respected as keepers of wisdom. While we need to learn from younger people in our rapidly changing context, respecting the insights of elders heals both church and society.

A respected Manitoba indigenous leader, Jules Lavallee, speaks freely about the impact an older man had on him during his youth. At the time, Jules was living on the streets and making poor choices. The elder told him to start each day by saying *Megwetch*—"thank-you," or "I give you all my gifts"—four times, once facing each direction. He was to repeat this throughout the day. Doing this gradually changed Jules' attitude. His grandmother also taught him to start each day by looking at the sun and saying *Megwetch* to *Manitou*—the name used to address the Great Spirit on the Canadian Plains.

As a young adult, Jules found employment as a life skills coach at *Oo-Za-We-Kwon* Training Centre. There he received teachings from many elders of different nations including Dakota (Sioux), Cree, and Ojibway. Jules is passing on the blessings he received from those elders. In 1994, he and his wife, Margaret, opened Red Willow Lodge, a traditional teaching and healing facility. Jules also serves as elder-in-residence at Winnipeg's Red River College, where he can bless and encourage students.

Naming the Challenges

How can we, who are in the last third of life, equip ourselves as spiritual guides for those who are in the first third of life, whether or not they have chosen to follow Christ? We need to face three major challenges as we equip ourselves for this quest.

Challenge 1: Recognizing, tending, and sharing spirituality. Paying close attention to our spirituality may take a bit of practice, but it is a necessary prerequisite if we wish to provide guidance for those who are in earlier stages of life's journey. If we learn to share our faith experiences winsomely, children, youth, and young adults will want to know about the spiritual aspects of our lives.

Young people seek integrity and authenticity rather than conformity. This doesn't mean that we have to be canonized as saints to become spiritual guides, but it does mean that our lives must humbly and transparently reflect our journey with God and the reconciling gospel of Jesus Christ. It also means that we need to learn to speak comfortably and from personal experience about God's presence in our lives and in the world.

We must learn to recognize and name the many ways God is present in our lives. This is the kind of activity and language we've often reserved for pastors, so it may take a bit of practice. This book will explore some of the ways that God is present with us in everyday events from birth until death, shaping the overarching stories of our lives.

Unless we die suddenly, we have some choice in the way we approach end of life issues. Our choices can have a powerful effect on how younger people view the spiritual aspects of aging and death. None of us can predict when and how we will die, what our future physical condition will be, or whether or not we will maintain our lucidity, but we can proactively claim a positive outlook. We live in a society that tends to glorify youth and to deny the approach of death. We lock frail people away. That attitude makes it difficult to die well, yet those of us who have accompanied others on their final journey know that dying well has powerful potential for leaving a legacy of faith.

As grandparents, our quest to bless the young can lead to our own spiritual growth, which will help us to end our lives well. As part of the process, we may rediscover and reclaim scripture as personally relevant and life-giving. If this happens, we will be as blessed as the younger generation we seek to guide on the journey toward the one we worship as the Way, the Truth, and the Life.

Challenge 2: Learn how faith grows. Understanding how faith grows is something we expect of Christian Education specialists. However, those specialists may not relate to the young people about whom we are concerned. In an age where we can no longer rely on social structures and attitudes to promote Christianity, we need to learn how faith grows so that we can become deliberate faith nurturers. Many children live far away from their grandparents or may not have Christian grandparents. Seniors are called to reach out and bless those children by practicing the art of spiritual grandparenting and passing on a legacy of faith.

Developments in psychology, brain science, and spirituality studies over the past fifty years have provided new and helpful tools to assist us in this holy task. *Please Pass the Faith* introduces some of those tools. It briefly summarizes how faith tends to express itself and develop in the young. At the same time, it speaks to the dynamic dance between development and conversion, between predictable maturation and the growth that results from unpredictable encounters with the Holy.

Challenge 3: Tap the spiritual potential of family stories and holiday celebrations. Stories and holidays share a marvellous ability to communicate faith and ideas across age boundaries. Therefore, we will look at the stories and themes in our lives that connect with our natural spiritual rhythms. We'll find out how they link with the underlying stories and themes of God's people through the ages. This book suggests activities that foster story-telling and story-listening in ways that sensitize us to God's presence in our lives and in the lives of the young, who may or may not see themselves as followers of Jesus.

Holiday celebrations often span generational divides. They present opportunities to connect with biblical themes addressing the core of our human experiences. When we engage these themes in fresh and personal ways, they help us to claim our place in God's ongoing story.

Conclusion

Our quest to spiritually mentor the young can lead to rediscovering and reclaiming Scripture as personally relevant and life-giving. Learning about the way faith changes as we mature helps us to find our own places on the journey of faith and life. The stories and celebrations that we tap for their spiritual potential allow us to place our stories within God's big story.

If these things happen as we practice and learn the art of spiritual grandparenting, we will be richly blessed indeed, even as we become a greater blessing to the young.

Reflection and Discussion Questions

1. Which descriptions of today's younger seniors resonated with you? How is your reality different?

2

Recognizing, Tending, and Sharing Spirituality

Finally, as we grow older, when we begin the last stages of life, it is clear that behaviours and failures are not the stuff of religion much anymore. Now, the ecstasy of life and the surrender to the Mystery become the last of the revelations of religion. Now, everything we learned long ago, gave up to some degree long ago, never left completely long ago, begins to make sense.[1]

How do we, as seniors, recognize and tend our own spirituality? Perhaps one of the first things we must do is to learn to accept with grace what we cannot change. And what is more unchangeable than that we will all die?

Accepting Mortality

Although it goes against the grain of today's society, coming to terms with our own mortality opens the door to greater spiritual awareness. Even so, it isn't easy to accept. Our culture upholds youthfulness

---

1. Joan Chittister, *The Gift of Years* (New York: Bluebridge, 2008), 103.

and tries to deny the inevitability of death. For instance, a growing abundance of magazines for seniors, such as *Zoomer*[2], are full of tips for looking and feeling younger than one is. Seniors can be as tempted as any adolescent by the unrealistic images of beauty promoted by the marketing industry. That leads to confusion, depression, and a denial of our bodies' natural decline.

On the other hand, if we accept mortality as a natural process, we can still claim our aging bodies as blessed and reflective of God's image. As John Enns, a wise senior in my congregation, once noted in our church newsletter, "This exceptional and superb piece of creation, subjected to relentless decay and perpetual regeneration, suffers loss of faculties and physical capabilities as, in advancing years, the rate of cellular destruction gradually exceeds the rate of repair."[3]

If we graciously accept the changes that are going on in our bodies, perhaps we can help younger people deal with their body image issues. This will prepare them for their own journey into adulthood and seniorhood, and teach them to embrace the gifts that will become theirs at each stage of life.

Seniors who recognize their reduced capacity and voluntarily downsize from homes to apartments to assisted living accommodations, or otherwise choose to do less, seem to enjoy a greater quality of life for a longer period of time. Those who embrace

2. *Zoomer*, published by CARP, the Canadian Association for retired persons, is a lifestyle magazine for men and women aged forty-five and older.

3. John Enns, "Reflections on Aging," in *The Grapevine*, ed. Larry Kehler (Winnipeg: Charleswood Mennonite Church, January, 2007), 6.

aging, living each day as a gift, live better lives than those who seek to deny it.

Lyndsay Green, a sociologist who has interviewed many grandparents, agrees. She has also learned that "to age successfully, instead of fighting to stay young, we should embrace aging. To stay attractive to others, we need to spend more time focusing on our inner selves, and less time having facelifts and hair implants."[4]

The spiritual disciplines involved in aging successfully focus on the gifts of faith and the essence of our being, rather than on staying young and active. This direction is stressed by Dosia Carlson, who has worked with many older adults. She maintains that responding to God's love and focusing on the gifts of the Spirit helps us to develop ever deeper, stronger roots, which empower us to share those gifts with others.[5]

Aging includes dealing with many losses. Physical agility and declining energy pose a significant loss that may be hard to accept as a gift, yet suffering can be a great teacher on days when we are able to learn. But what about those days when the loss and suffering of declining health tower over everything else in our lives? Can love dominate our fear over decline? Does anticipating such decline lead to discouragement and despair? Or can it help us gratefully accept, as a gift, any remaining health and time? And finally, what does this deterioration do to our roles as grandparents? Can we still be spiritual guides as we move from active *doing* to frailer states of *being*?

---

4. Lyndsay Green, *You could live a really long time: are you ready?* (Toronto: Thomas Allen Publishers, 2010), 19.

5. Dosia Carlson, *Engaging in Ministry with Older Adults* (Herndon: Alban Institute, 1997), 6.

Authors James C. Fisher and Henry C. Simmons state that "Aging is not for sissies; it is for those with indomitable and grateful spirits."[6] Such a spirit is a gift which can be recognized with gratitude. Like other spiritual gifts, it is one we can prepare ourselves to receive by consciously practicing the spiritual disciplines of resilient hope and gratitude. Learning to do this at an early age will help people grow into seniors who inspire others.

Practicing hope, gratitude, and the desire to let God's blessings flow through us toward others—even as we think realistically about the natural process of aging, which leads toward death—prepares us to die well. It can also shape us into winsome elderly seniors who continue to attract and inspire our grandchildren. While some of us will have our lives cut short suddenly though an accident or a health crisis, many of us will have the opportunity to approach death more gradually. We can use that time to prepare and to provide spiritual guidance for our children and grandchildren, and for others to whom we relate— like the staff in hospitals and personal care homes.

Fisher and Simmons share Henry Nouwen's counsel for this season to "trust that the time ahead . . . will be the most important time of your life, not just for you, but for all of us whom you love and who love you."[7]

In a similar vein, Joan Chittister maintains that seniors teach us how to die, as well as how to live. They teach us "how to make sense of the unity between life and death, how to love life without

---

6. James C. Fisher, Henry C. Simmons, *A Journey Called Aging: Challenges and Opportunities in Older Adulthood* (New York: Best Business Books, 2007), 142.

7. Ibid., 166.

fearing death—*because we know ourselves to have been always on the way, even when we did not know where we were going.*"[8]

I have had the privilege of accompanying several family members as they approached death. Those last days of earthly life are a holy time when many personal differences recede. The veil of separation between earth and heaven grows thin. New and inspiring aspects of a loved one's faith become apparent, resulting in deep blessing. One aunt, from whom I had previously only heard a prayer of table grace, blessed me deeply with moving and perceptive intercessory prayers for my children when I came to visit her in the cancer ward. She had the strength of spirit to love life without fearing death. She sensed herself on the journey toward greater understanding of her purpose and an even more complete union with the Creator.

Chittister describes the last revelations of religion as an embrace of the ecstasy of life and surrender to the Mystery. As we surrender to this mystery, everything we have learned over our lifespan is integrated and begins to make sense, and helps us move toward a new beginning with God in eternity.[9]

May it be so with us.

She also writes, "We leave behind, in our very positions on death and life, on purpose and meaning, a model of our relationship with God. Our own spiritual life is both a challenge and a support to the spiritual struggles of those around us. As they themselves approach the moment of truth, like us, they look for models of what it means to go beyond speculation, despite uncertainty."[10]

---

8. Chittister, *The Gift of Years*, 103. Emphasis mine.

9. Ibid., 104.

10. Ibid., 217.

It is so encouraging to think that even when our rational faculties weaken, our spiritual faculties can surface to sustain us and inspire those who are with us in our dying. If we are fortunate enough to have contact with our grandchildren at that time, we trust that our dying well can inspire them.

If we can grow to be such grandparents and great grandparents, the young people who are dear to us and the church that is our spiritual home will be deeply blessed.

Tending Our Faith

In a seminar about young seniors and faith, I asked participants to indicate which spiritual practices currently nurtured their faith. Their responses included reflective, private activities like reading and meditating on scripture or other spiritual writing; practicing stillness and solitude; self-examination and confession; seeking and granting forgiveness; journaling; and fasting. They also included physical practices such as honouring their bodies, honouring the Sabbath, living simply, caring for creation, singing, offering hospitality, and prayer.

In addition, there were corporate practices or things we do together as Christians such as sharing our faith stories, speaking the truth in love, discerning Scripture and God's will, engaging in service projects, fellowship and communal care, worship, and celebration.

From this list of responses, participants selected the five activities they found most sustaining at their present stage of life. Then they reflected on the practices that they felt would sustain them as they aged and became frail. While there was a definite overlap of meaningful practices between stages, lists for the present included more physical and communal activities. Lists for the future revealed a greater focus on reflective, private disciplines.

The exercise led to a healthy discussion about how we can age gracefully and spiritually. While our expressions of spirituality are as unique as our personalities, they share a common rhythmic blend of caring conversation, devotions, service, rituals, and traditions. The kinds of activities composing this rhythm adapt to reflect our place along life's journey.

Which of the spiritual practices listed above belong to your own favoured five? And which of these practices would the young people in your life choose? If you would like to explore them further, resources abound in Christian bookstores and on Christian websites.

Whether we deliberately practice spiritual disciplines or participate in them more randomly and intuitively, our spiritual lives have a rhythm that is as natural as breath and heartbeat. Our personal spiritual rhythm, closely linked to our emotions, is probably most evident in the ways we manage our concerns and joys. When we rejoice, how do we share that joy with God and others? When we learn something new, how do we integrate that knowledge into our worldview? When we are troubled, how do we lament, how do we share our sorrows, and how do we meet God in those shadow places? When we see a need, how do we respond? Do we see ourselves as partners in God's mission? Our responses to questions such as these shape our spiritual rhythms.

Individuals can learn to identify their own rhythmic spirituality with the help of a spiritual director, a person who is trained to accompany others on such a journey. In a congregational resource, *The Wisdom of the Seasons*,[11] author Charles Olsen writes that spiritual directors encourage their directees to look for three basic movements in their lives: *letting go, naming God's presence, and taking hold of God's presence.*

Even if we have never met with a spiritual director, we can benefit from seeking our personal spiritual rhythm within these categories. As we gain familiarity with this rhythm in our experiences, we become better acquainted with our spiritual stories. Our vocabulary for talking about spiritual matters grows, making it easier for us to serve as spiritual guides who can both "walk the talk," and "talk the walk."

Movement 1: Letting go. The movement of *letting go* is something with which seniors are very familiar. If we retired from the paid work force, we have let go of the status and community that were part of that lifestyle. That surrender, with all of its benefits and losses, shapes us.

And then there is the kind of letting go that belongs to the natural family life cycle. We experience this as our children move from dependence upon us to independence. Expecting obedience from adult children may bring disappointment—and confrontation with the reality that we have little control in their lives. If we are wise enough to release our expectations for obedience and assume a consulting role instead, communication lines may remain open. Our adult children may even seek our advice occasionally.

On the other hand, there is a form of letting go that comes from family strife. Perhaps our children

---

11. Charles Olsen, *The Wisdom of the Seasons: How the Church Year Helps Us Understand Our Congregational Stories* (Herndon: Alban Institute, 2009), 4.

have not lived up to our dreams for them. If so, we may need to free ourselves from those dreams to embrace reality. Perhaps conflict and broken relationships damaged family life, creating dysfunction and hurt. We may need to temporarily release goals for family harmony and intimacy in order to love family members from a distance until they, or we, are ready to reconnect more positively. A marriage breakup or the death of a spouse challenges us to accept another kind of surrender. Some of us may need to let go of children or grandchildren who are incarcerated, or cannot safely be allowed into our homes. Perhaps we're not allowed to visit them. For some of us, hopes for grandchildren may have been dashed by infertility issues, or by our children's same sex orientation.

Whether or not our families experience such conflict and loss, by the time we become seniors, all of us will encounter stressful situations where letting go is necessary. It allows us to move beyond conflict and on to new life-affirming realities. Whatever life has dealt us, we've probably looked loss in the eye. After doing so, we may see life more clearly, identify our priorities, form new friendships, and grow from the experience.

Letting go does have potential downsides. Involuntary experiences of loss may actually tempt us to lose hope, as do observations of the sadness, violence, senseless destruction, and self-centered cruelty around and within us. We need to let go in the awareness of God's presence, remembering that "a bruised reed he will not break, and a dimly burning wick he will not quench" (Isaiah 42: 3).

As we age, our bodies demand that we free ourselves from earlier expectations of them. If we redefine those expectations to suit the realities of declining muscle strength and stamina, we will live better lives than if we succumb to the lure of ads about staying eternally young. We won't occupy our time with futile attempts to defy nature. Accepting our new realities and releasing inappropriate expectations may actually free our spirits of unnecessary baggage for the remainder of life's journey.

The challenges of learning to let go are not new to any senior, but naming them sets the stage for recognizing the presence of God within each. To tap into the spiritual value of these challenges, it helps to remember that God has also let go. By giving humans free will, God showed us that authentic relationships are based on the freedom to commit, or not. By allowing Jesus, God's Son, to live with humans and to die in a brutal crucifixion, God sacrificially let go so that humanity might know salvation.

This divine surrender is perhaps captured best in Philippians 2:6-8, part of a passage which is often referred to as the Christ Hymn. Paul wrote that Christ Jesus, "who, though he was in the form of God, did not regard equality with God as something to be exploited, but emptied himself, taking the form of a slave, being born in human likeness. And being found in human form, he humbled himself and became obedient to the point of death—even death on a cross."

Just as this surrender is only the first part of that amazing hymn of the early church, it is only the first step in the rhythm of our spiritual lives. Claiming this process, which is so often fraught with pain, is an essential part of living spiritually. It helps us to yield with some measure of grace. Learning to let go includes surrendering our yearnings and losses to the love of God. We may fear that it will reduce us to insignificance, but when we do "let go and let God," blessings result.

I have learned and relearned this lesson several times. Sometimes my adult children make choices that contradict the advice I would give, if asked. At such times I tend to worry, fret, pray, and then worry some more. When I release these anxieties and trust God to work in their lives through other people, I am frequently surprised. I've experienced personal inner growth and I've witnessed how my young adult children are influenced positively by others.

Just as God exalted Jesus for his humble sacrifice, God honours our acts of surrender by taking over and helping our spirits grow. While we need to hold on to core parts of our identity, there are other attitudes, relationships, and habits to which we are called to say good-bye so that God can help us grow. May God grant us the wisdom to know the difference!

Movement 2: Naming God's presence. Whose spirits have not been moved to praise by sunrises or sunsets? Imagine gold- or pink-hued light filtering through the irregular lacework of tree branches stretching toward the Creator, while being deeply rooted in the soil. Psalm 8 provides us with a wonderful example of praising the presence of God in creation. We join in with psalmist in verse 1, "Oh, Lord, our Sovereign, how majestic is your name in all the earth!"

The many miracles of nature—green sprouts transforming into plants with fruit on the vine, panoramic vistas of mountains, starry skies—remind us of the inscrutable and wise provisions of our Creator. Whether we observe these wonders as part of a large plan or experience them as personal gifts of encouragement or challenge, creation helps us to see the presence of God in the world.

Do we remember to name and celebrate these as gifts of God with the young people in our lives?

We also learn to notice the presence of God through the experiences of others. Several years ago my congregation sang the hymn, "Precious Lord, take my hand," under the leadership of Lindsay Robinson, an African-American minister from south-eastern U.S. He introduced the hymn by telling us how he regularly visualized Jesus walking right next to him when he sang it. I will probably never think about that song again without remembering Lindsay's testimony. This is just one example of experiencing Jesus as Immanuel, as God with us.

Can we name examples of seeing the presence of God with us in the relationships that fill our days? During my years as an elementary school teacher, I frequently challenged myself to look for the image of God in my students, especially in those I found harder to love. When students were defiant or uncooperative, I would gaze into their eyes and search for reflections of Christ. This helpful exercise redeemed many trying moments.

At other times, helpful gestures from a student, a colleague, or a parent volunteer reminded me of God's loving accompaniment in my life. I will never forget the faithfulness of my students' prayers for my husband when his work took him on a long trip to the Democratic Republic of Congo during a time of political unrest.

To notice the presence of God with and among us, we need only tune in to everyday events and relationships with receptive, Spirit-led eyes. Is God speaking to us through the trusting love or probing questions of a grandchild?

Tuning in to the presence of God in our relationships happens more easily if we practice becoming quiet, and listen for the still small voice of God within us. Many spiritual practices such as centering prayer, the devotional reading of Scripture, journaling, singing, playing, or listening to spiritual music will help us do so.

An increasing number of Protestants, including Mennonites, go on guided spiritual retreats or engage in spiritual friendships and spiritual direction to become familiar with recognizing God at work in their lives. These practices have a long history within the religious life of the Catholic denomination, but now they serve a widening spectrum of Christians and lay people, often through Catholic retreat centres.

We experience the awareness of God in and among us in many ways. We may feel an encouraging and comforting awareness deep within, a sense of accompaniment, a sense of affirmation or nudging, or an inner turmoil that motivates us to make a needed change.

While some people feel closest to God when they are still and praying, others feel most aware of God when they exert themselves physically. Children, youth, and younger men often feel most spiritually alive when they are active. When I teach Sunday school to preschoolers, I invite them into a short period of active prayer where they show God how high they can jump or how fast they can run. They love it! I believe God smiles as they demonstrate the goodness and energy of the bodies they've been given. Similarly, when I care for my preschool grandchildren, I make sure they have chances to run. As they do, I casually comment about how thankful I am for the good legs and healthy bodies God has given them.

Action-oriented spiritual practices for adults include activities such as weeding, processing vegetables, building furniture, sculpting, jogging, sorting food at a food bank, and caring for infants in the church nursery. Consider praying the Lord's Prayer as you swim or water garden plants. In the latter activity, how dry the ground is determines how many plants are included with each recitation.

The shift from activity to quiet time can also be a holy experience. When an infant or toddler falls asleep in the arms or care of a loving grandparent, both grandparent and child enter into a holy zone where God's presence is palpable.

Some learn to regard life's interruptions as times when God's Spirit is nudging them to listen and respond. People drop in unexpectedly. A family member is hospitalized. Suddenly, the day is disrupted. We find ourselves in a significant exchange with hospital staff or with a stranger in the waiting room. When we learn to accept these encounters as opportunities sent to us by God, they become less frustrating and we become more aware of God's activity in our world.

We can also learn to recognize the presence of the Holy Spirit in our agitation over things that we feel are not as they should be. This agitation or holy discontent moves us toward needed change. When we are most upset about the dynamics at work or in our families, the fire in our bellies burns hot enough to force us into re-evaluation.

For me, one such period of agitation grew from increasing stress around our Christmas family gathering. We typically got together on Christmas Eve, but as the family grew and preparations became more complex, it interfered with my desire to be part of our congregation's Christmas Eve program. Although change was difficult to initiate, we began to hold our family gatherings at another time. They have been at least as rich as our earlier celebrations. This shift makes a statement that, at least for this season in life, family celebration need not displace congregational worship. Through it, I sensed the continued activity of the Holy Spirit in my family, just as I now recognize the Spirit's presence in the agitation that led to the change.

We can sense and learn to name the presence of God within the warmth and excitement of celebration. Celebrations often link us across generations and provide great opportunities for naming the goodness of God's presence within and among us. Our family is gradually replacing a Christmas gift-giving tradition with one of sharing stories with each other. In 2011, I asked each of my children and grandchildren for a written account of an experience they want to remember. I will look for the God moments in each of these stories, whether the teller recognizes it as such or not. As opportunities arise, especially with those who are not resisting God's presence, I will share how I see God at work in their lives through those stories.

Because we are created in God's image, we rely on the Holy Spirit to help us notice God in us. This happens whenever we live in ways that align with the divine image, which exists in a rich community of Creator, Redeemer, and Sustainer. This threefold aspect of God parallels our awareness of the divine as God above us, God with us, and God within us.[12] While we arrive at an awareness of God within us in many ways, this naming of God's presence in our lives helps us move into the final part of our spiritual rhythm, that of taking hold.

Movement 3: Taking hold of God's presence. When we recognize God's presence in the process of letting go and learn to name God's presence in our lives, we are naturally led to take hold of God's presence—to

---

12. Ibid., 46.

respond to it—by active involvement in God's mission in the world.[13]

Practical and service oriented Christians may not always notice God at work in their service projects. Sometimes we view service as simply doing what is needed in a hurting world, but celebrating it as part of our spiritual rhythm enriches the gifts we receive in helping others. This occurs whether or not we articulate it as serving in the name of Christ.

This is an area where we can allow younger generations to nurture us. Young people who work at summer camps, participate in short term mission trips, or engage in creation care projects such as urban farming often refer to ways these experiences shape them spiritually.

Service experiences abound and are certainly not just for youth—they are also common among healthy seniors. Within the Mennonite tradition, many seniors choose to serve with Mennonite Disaster Service (MDS), Service Opportunities for Older People (SOOP), in local ministries, or with other service agencies. Not only do such projects respond to world needs in partnership with God's mission, they also provide meaningful friendships and focus for retired seniors who are faced with reorganizing their lives after paid employment ends.

In addition, some congregations plan intergenerational service trips. Such trips bring blessing through the service they provide for others and through intergenerational relationships that deepen as multiple age groups serve, reflect, and report on God's presence in the activities they do together.

Frequently, those who are assisted by service projects bless volunteers by helping them to see how

---

13. Ibid., 7.

God is present in their activities. Carmen, a woman from the Gulf Coast of Mississippi whose home was destroyed by Hurricane Katrina, watched despondently as the MDS crew rebuilt her house. All the while, her ten-year-old son prayed. He asked her if she was saying her prayers, too. When the crew worked continuously on a particularly wet and miserable day, Carmen suddenly realised how much love was going into the project and her faith returned.

Pam Driedger's booklet, *Beyond our Fears: Following Jesus in Times of Crisis*, shares Carmen's reflection on the experience. "That's when I got my faith back. . . . I came to love those people. They were my bits and pieces to put my life back together and make me know that there is a God and whatever happens, he's going to fix it . . . Now I speak at lots of different events, not to get help for me, but to get help for other people . . . I have never felt the need to help others as much as I do now."[14]

God was definitely revealed to Carmen through the MDS project and is now present in her advocacy work. But the MDS volunteers who received Carmen's testimony were also blessed by knowing how God worked through their efforts.

Seeing God at work in our projects can happen close to home, too. Chapter Three will focus on learning to claim and name God's presence in more personal stories.

---

14. Pam Driedger, *Beyond our Fears: Following Jesus in Times of Crisis* (Scottdale/Waterloo: Faith and Life Resources, 2009), 11–12. This adult curriculum was written to help people prepare for a pandemic and other crisis. It includes a leader's guide and can be purchased from MennoMedia at http://store.mpn.net/productdetails.cfm?PC=1183.

Life as a River-Story: A Big Picture Exercise

We see God as we let go and when we name God's presence in our experience. We take hold of God's presence by responding to it and participating in God's mission in the world. These rhythms help us develop sensors for God's presence above us, with us, and within us. Our encounter with the Holy can be seen in all these individual parts. This is especially true if participation in congregational disciplines of worship, prayer, and study anchor us in the long line of witnesses who have also seen God at work in their lives.

Observing our personal big picture story provides yet another rewarding and inspiring perspective. As our days grow in number and our storehouse of experiences fills up, we come to see God's presence in the past, even if we didn't recognize it at the time. The following exercise, first recommended for use with teenage girls by Joyce Mercer[15], can also equip seniors to see God's presence throughout their longer view of life.

Using a pen or pencil, a piece of paper, and as much time as you need, reflect on your life. Draw it as a river with bends, twists, and turns to reflect the major events of your life. Label each curve. Your river could include recollections such as:

- your earliest memories of sensing the Holy;
- worship experiences that left a special imprint on your soul;
- times of testing and claiming beliefs;

---

15. Joyce Mercer, *GirlTalk/GodTalk* (San Francisco: Jossey Bass, 2008), 123.

- the time you chose Christ and Christ's church as the center of your life;
- encounters with specific guiding Scriptures;
- formative experiences of sharing the journey with saints and sinners;
- growth in your understanding of what it means to be "in Christ;"
- hard experiences and doubts; and
- times of blessing others and being blessed.

Once you've done this, travel along the river again and ask yourself about the people who were significant along the journey. Add their names to the appropriate places.

Finally, take another look at these events and names, and reflect on how God was present. When did God seem near to you? When did God seem distant?

This activity has the potential to reveal God's presence in our lives for great personal benefit. It might even provide an outline for writing memoirs, whether we place ourselves within the grand narrative of the biblical/church story or not. God is active everywhere. No matter where we find ourselves, this tool can make it easier to talk spiritually with others by providing common entry points for spiritual reflection.

Conclusion

In this chapter we looked at seniors' spirituality from many different angles. Some aspects of spiritual growth or understanding still await us, while others already feel familiar. Together they create the multi-faceted jewel of faith that emerges as we grow older in Christ—or as we allow Christ to increasingly form us as we age.

Although it goes against the grain of today's society, coming to terms with our own mortality opens the door to greater spiritual awareness. We learn to accept aging and mortality so that we are able to age well, to engage in the discipline of making deliberate choices that will tend and shape our spiritual lives before we become frail. We can begin to make these choices by exploring the classic themes of *letting go*, *naming God's presence*, and *taking hold of God's presence*. By trusting God, noticing how God is active in our lives, and responding to that presence by taking part in God's mission in the world, we recognize the entirety of our lives as a journey with God and with God's people through the ages. Understanding these spiritual rhythms allows us to navigate future joys, concerns, and even disruptions, with a greater awareness of God's presence and leading. By doing so, we learn to recognize and tend spirituality—and we develop the ability to share our faith with others in a tangible way.

Reflection and Discussion Questions

Accepting our mortality

1. How does or could accepting your mortality impact your spiritual health? Why are we so afraid of life's final chapter? If you are not sure, prepare or review your will.
2. What stories of seniors who have died well give you courage and wisdom for facing your own death? Share these stories with each other.
3. How do you respond to the idea that our final days are the most important days of our lives?
4. Even when we have dementia, God works within us to prepare our souls for a homecoming. If

you have accompanied a person with dementia, share with others what you have learned.

5. How does dying well relate to our calling as
   spiritual guides for the young?

Letting go

1. What spiritual practices are most helpful for
   your current stage on the journey of faith?
   How do they compare to those of a young person you care about?
2. What place does letting go have in your spiritual health?
3. What are you called to let go of?
4. What experiences of letting go can you claim as
   part of your walk with God?
5. What biblical stories of letting go can assist
   you in this frequently painful process?

Noticing and naming God's presence

1. What are your responses to thinking about
   noticing and naming the presence of God as
   part of our spirituality?
2. During what activities are you most aware of
   God's presence?
3. In what places are you most aware of God's
   presence?

Taking hold of God's presence

1. What are your thoughts about taking hold of
   God's presence, or responding to it, as part of
   your spirituality?
2. During what activities do you find yourself
   becoming aware of God's presence and God's
   dream for the world?
3. How can you give these activities an inter-generational dimension?

Life as a river-story

1. How might such an exercise be used in a seniors' fellowship group in your congregation or with neighbours or family members?
2. What aspects of your life "river-story" might open the way for conversations about the spiritual in life with older grandchildren?

3

How Does Faith Grow?

As Christian seniors and grandparents, one of our deepest desires is for our children and grandchildren to be in a life-giving, saving relationship with God. But we also know, sometimes from painful personal experience, that we can obstruct that process.

Take this example from Grandma Nancy's life. When she prayed aloud at the extended family supper table for her three year old granddaughter, Megan, to grow to know and love the Lord, Megan was upset. Later, Megan drew her mother aside to say that her beloved Grandma Nancy had just prayed a dumb prayer.

"Oh really," her mother responded, "and what did you think was dumb about it?"

"Well, Mommy, I already know and love God! I don't need to grow up first."

We don't want to erect barriers between children and God. Nor did Grandma Nancy. Thankfully, Megan was able to process what happened with her mother, who understood that faith is alive and well in children long before they can reason and articulate their beliefs.

It is sobering to realize how easily we can hurt our grandchildren's spiritual growth, even as we try to nurture it.

This true vignette—with names changed to protect privacy—must not discourage us from praying aloud for and with our grandchildren, or from
engaging them in spiritual conversations. Rather,
it is an encouragement to learn about the process
of faith development. Equipping ourselves with a
primer in faith formation and children's spirituality allows us to step more confidently into the awe-
filled and holy role of faith journey guides for the
young. Our life experience allows us to share language and practices that help them to express their
awareness of God. And they, in turn, can offer us
fresh perspectives on precious truths that may have
become somewhat stale for us.[1]

We are blessed with wonderful tools for understanding and supporting faith in children. Over the
last fifty years or so, psychologists and Christian
educators have collaborated to understand how
faith grows and to develop theories and other tools
that will help us appreciate it. In the last thirty years
or so, additional researchers and practitioners in the
social sciences and brain science have joined that
effort, creating the new interdisciplinary field, children's spirituality studies. New theologies of childhood are attempting to describe the mystery of the
Holy Spirit's outpouring of grace.

Let's read these theologies with a critical eye.
While each child's journey with the Holy is unique,
analytical tools provide valuable insights about how
human maturation shapes the spiritual journey.
This chapter introduces a theology of childhood,

---

1. Elsie Rempel, *Forming Faith: Prayer Journeys with Children*
(Winnipeg: Mennonite Church Canada, 2009). This resource
includes many suggestions for praying with and for children and
is available for download. www.mennonitechurch.ca/tiny/1133.

and offers key gleanings from the work of faith formation specialists. If this brief and anecdotal introduction inspires you to learn more, the footnotes throughout the book will lead you to other resources with more detailed treatments of the topic.

Children Are Members of God's Family

As children's spirituality studies show, the church holds unformulated, conflicted views about children and about appropriate ways of participating in their spiritual formation. Author, children's spirituality specialist, and practical theologian Jerome Berryman states, "Ambivalent feelings about children are deeply held, both a high and a low value."[2]

A child's faith is important, but it differs distinctively from an adult's faith. So how can we best support spiritual growth in children?

Previously, children were filled with information about God before they were considered capable of faith. Now, children are viewed as pilgrims on a spiritual journey that begins in the womb. They are precious members of the family of God, whether or not they have been baptized into the body of Christ.

As a teacher who led children in daily morning worship for a number of years, I gained a deep appreciation for the faith of children. The theology of children explored here evolved from that practical experience, along with constructive conversations with my denominational tradition, and the broader work taking place in the area of children's spirituality.

2. Jerome Berryman, "Children and Mature Spirituality," in *Children's Spirituality: Christian Perspectives, Research and Applications*, ed. Donald Ratcliff (Eugene: Cascade Books, 2004), 22–41.

The dominant voices in this area of study come from mainline churches where infant baptism is typical, especially for the children of churchgoing families. My theological understanding of the role and place of children in the family of God is grounded in the Anabaptist theology of the Mennonite denomination, which is often referred to as the "believers church" tradition. In this tradition, children are accepted as part of the family of God from birth, but they are not baptized and they do not become members of the church—the Body of Christ—until they are believers who freely declare their faith as adolescents or adults.

Concepts of Children's Faith

Children are spiritual beings with gifts that reflect their unique place in the family of God. We may think of them as members of the body of Christ, as is the case when they are baptized as infants. Or we may view them as part of the family of God in the believers church tradition. Whichever perspective we embrace, we can and must learn from children in ways that acknowledge both their spiritual and developmental gifts.

Five key concepts shape the theology of children's faith upon which this book is based:

Concept 1: Children have a privileged spot on the lap of Jesus. Children are gifts and belong to God's kingdom (Matthew 18:1-4, 19:13-15; Mark 10:13-16; Luke 18:15-17). Jesus welcomed and blessed them when his disciples wanted to send them away.

If we follow Jesus' example, children will also have a privileged spot on our laps and on the metaphorical lap of the congregation. God has entrusted them to us with the mandate to nurture them for the purposes of God. We dare not leave them to be lured into the purposes of the world, which works hard at shaping their identity through the advertizing industry and other pervasive media. This is a special test for grandparents, who love to thrill their grandchildren with the gifts they desire—gifts that may be promoted by advertisers and have little to do with faith or living God's way.

Concept 2: Children's faith contributes to the vitality of faith communities. Consider how grandchildren contribute to multi-generational family life. A new grandchild helps a family *be* a family by basking in the love of the generations and meeting caregivers' needs to give care. As the child matures, he or she continues to contribute to the health and welfare of the family in ways that are appropriate to age and giftings.

As we learn to integrate children into congregational life, their gifts will contribute to the life of congregations in similar ways. My congregation's worship grows richer as we invite children to serve in worship as ushers or scripture readers or to extend the call to worship. Both families and congregations are blessed and gifted whenever they embrace, bless, teach, worship with, and learn from the children to whom the kingdom of God belongs.

Concept 3: Children possess a complex innocence and develop their moral and spiritual accountability gradually. Children mature towards increasing levels of accountability, both morally and spiritually. Menno Simons, after whom Mennonites are named, challenged traditional sixteenth-century perceptions of original sin with his understanding of children's complex innocence. He did this to explain that children did not require infant baptism to be saved. He argued that children are protected by God's grace and enjoy God's favour until they are mature enough to understand what following Christ means, and then knowingly accept or reject Christ.

Today the vocabulary and issues surrounding children's spiritual status are expanding beyond concerns for their salvation. They now address their growing levels of ability to make decisions and take responsibility. Children's levels of moral and spiritual responsibility and accountability develop gradually. It is reassuring to know that as this happens, children are under the protection of God's grace.

Concept 4: Young children can relate to a God who is hidden yet wants to be found. This perspective of God may appear somewhat unusual to adults. We may understand it by observing the children in our lives whose game of hide-and-seek reflects this tension. Hide-and-seek invites children into the pleasurable idea of something secret—the act of hiding. But even as they hide, they want the other players to find them so that they can return to their place in the group or community.

Children's social, emotional, and intellectual maturation is reflected in this activity. At first they will take cues for their actions from the voices and expressions of those around them. Over time they begin to recognize both their separateness and their connection with family and community. They progress to evaluating situations from another person's perspective.[3] They learn to consider, "What

---

3. Laura E. Berk, *Child Development*, Canadian ed. (Toronto: Pearson Education Canada, 2003) 406–7, 469–70.

place can I find to hide where she won't think of looking for me?"

When we have fun playing hide-and-seek with the young we help them develop spiritually as well as socially. Theologian Jerome Berryman writes, "It is essential to human nature and to developing healthy relationships with each other and with God."[4]

What if God is a God of hiddenness, as described in the book of Isaiah, "Truly you are a God who hides himself, a God of Israel, the Savior" (45:15)?

Bob Haverluck, Manitoba theologian, cartoonist, and artist, writes, "I believe God is hidden but wants to be found. God is playing, as it were. Tirelessly playing hide-and-seek . . . Life, it seems, is so serious to the Holy, that we must stop not playing."[5]

Could this be part of what Jesus meant when he said, "Unless you change and become like children, you will never enter the kingdom of heaven" (Matthew 18:3)? Perhaps it is. After all, Jesus is also quoted as saying "Seek, and you shall find" (Matthew 7:7).

Some children and adults protect their lives by hiding to escape domestic violence or political and social upheaval. They connect with the hidden nature of God differently. They may view God as one who helps them remain hidden, or as one who cries with them as they tremble in fear.

---

4. Jerome Berryman, "Children and Mature Spirituality," in *Children's Spirituality: Christian Perspectives, Research and Applications*, ed. Donald Ratcliff (Eugene: Cascade Books, 2004), 22–41. Berryman's essay includes hide-and-seek as a major component of his theology. He adds, on page 24, that this idea has been dignified in theology by the Latin phrase, *Deus Absconditus atque Praesens* (God is hidden yet also present).

5. Bob Haverluck, "Hiding and Seeking God: A Wordly Art", in *ARTS: The Arts in Religious and Theological Studies*, 18.1. (2006), 18–25.

*Concept 5: Children's spiritual awareness is intrin-
sic—deeply rooted and intuitively sensed—but also
developmentally sensitive.* As the upcoming section
on primal faith will illustrate, children are innately
spiritual, but their spirituality is also developmentally sensitive. Their awareness needs to be nurtured
by instruction, by encouragement to wonder about
life and God, and through participation in the
worship and mission practices of our families and
congregations.

As children participate in actions of worship
and service, they develop a spiritual toolbox that
includes vocabulary, symbols, and actions. Faith
grows best in children when teaching and preaching
is combined with activities like worship that encourage encounters with God.

As children mature, their understanding of spiritual practices deepens, especially if they are included
in worship and mission and are familiar with related
musical and symbolic actions. For instance, consider
children who serve at a food bank as soon as they
are physically able to be helpful. This experience
allows them to respond on a deeper level to the hospitality of Jesus at the tables where they gather, particularly when they are introduced to the language
and actions that acknowledge Jesus as host.

These five key concepts about the gifts of children's faith form a foundation for the coming section about the stages of child faith development.
Here, in point form, is a summary of these concepts
for easy reference:

1. Children have a privileged spot on the lap of
   Jesus and the church.
2. Children's faith contributes to the vitality of
   faith communities.

3. Children possess a complex innocence and develop their moral and spiritual accountability gradually.
4. Young children can relate to a God who is hidden yet wants to be found.
5. Children's spiritual awareness is intrinsic—deeply rooted and intuitively sensed—but also developmentally sensitive.

Stages of Faith Development

This section describes the process of faith development through different periods of childhood for those who grow up in Christian families and attend church. Those who are introduced to faith later in life move through most of the earlier stages in this process quickly, with more mature minds and personalities. Your grandchildren may fit into both categories.

In his popular reference book, *Weaving the New Creation: Stages of Faith and the Public Church*, James W. Fowler describes faith stages as "a succession of ways of constructing and interpreting our experience of self, others, and the world in light of relatedness to God."[6] The stages of faith referred to in *Please Pass the Faith* are based upon Fowler's observations, but appropriate current developments and insights are also included.[7]

---

6. James W. Fowler, *Weaving the New Creation: Stages of Faith and the Public Church* (San Francisco: HarperSanFrancisco, 1991), 91. This book updates Fowler's theories in a previously published work; *Stages of Faith: The Psychology of Human Development and the Quest for Meaning* (New York: Harper Collins, 1981).

7. Two resources written by Robert J. Keeley are particularly helpful for reflecting on Fowler's theory from our current context: Robert J. Keeley, "Faith Development and Faith Formation: More than Just Ages and Stages," *Lifelong*

To illustrate how faith development can take shape in the very young, I'll draw from my experience with my grandchildren. One evening, as I babysat my three-year-old granddaughter, Sonya,[8] she picked up a Christmas card with the nativity scene on it. She asked me to sing the song out of this "book." I sang "Away in a Manger" for her and showed her some simple accompanying actions. She asked me to sing it with her repeatedly over the next few weeks.

At first Sonya imitated my actions. Soon that wasn't real enough. She became the "pretend Mary," and held the wooden Jesus from the Christmas crèche in her hands. When it was time for Jesus to "lay down his sweet head," she lay down on the floor with Jesus, just like her mom would lie down with her at nap time. Then she pointed out the stars in the bright sky to her baby, bent over him in a pose of adoration when I sang, "looked down where he lay," and snuggled in to sleep with him.

Current understandings of primal faith assume that the "hunger for a personal relation to God in which we feel ourselves to be known and loved in deep and comprehensive ways,"[9] which Fowler ascribed to later faith stages, are already experienced intuitively at early stages. This happens before a large vocabulary and the ability to think

---

Faith 4, no. 3 (2010): 20–27, and Robert J. Keeley, "Step by Step: Faith Development and Faith Formation," in *Shaped by God: Twelve Essentials for Nurturing Faith in Children, Youth, and Adults*, ed. Robert J. Keeley (Grand Rapids: Faith Alive Christian Resources, 2010), 59–70.

8. All names of family members have been changed to maintain privacy.

9. Fowler, *Weaving the New Creation*, 91.

in concepts become part of the child's toolbox for making sense of the world, as was illustrated by the anecdote about Sonya.

All of us are at different stages on a journey of faith formation. As Christians, we can claim with Paul, "All things have been created through [Christ] and for him . . . [and] in whom all things hold together" (Colossians 1:16b, 17b). We can claim that Christ is the center. We are all on a journey toward that center, whether we recognize it or not.[10]

Individual faith journeys differ widely. Because we see life most clearly from our own perspective, we can be tempted to consider our faith stage the norm, and use it to judge others. Therefore, as we begin this section, I invite you to spend a few moments remembering your faith as a child:

- What were the parts of the worship service, where were the specific places, and what were the activities that helped you worship and feel close to God?
- What can you remember about learning to pray or about learning the Bible stories for the first time?
- What do you remember about thinking like a child?

Whether you have these memories or not, I encourage you to spend some time with a child to learn what child faith is like. In the words of Bob Haverluck, "Because you lack the inexperience for the job of walking shorelines, take a child with you.

---

10. This idea need not impose Christian ideas on other religions, but it does claim that the spiritual journeys of other faiths are ultimately headed toward the same center.

The child will show you how to stop, go slow and be where water, earth and air meet."[11] That same child will show you where childhood and the Holy meet.

Perhaps the story of Sonya, above, and other stories shared here will trigger memories of the children you love and care for. Together with summarized research findings, these stories provide windows into the faith of children, youth, and emerging adults.

Primal Faith. According to Fowler, infants and toddlers who have yet to develop rational thinking are still capable of expressing an innate spirituality. They share several key characteristics:

- They are intuitively conscious of and trusting toward God.
- They sense great awe, wonder, and curiosity about the world.
- They respond to Jesus somewhat like they respond to a favourite stuffed toy or doll.
- They understand love as having ones' needs met.
- They experience their mother, or the primary caregiver, as "God with skin on."
- They distinguish between fantasy and reality with difficulty. Imaginary friends are common and seem real. Jesus and angels can be experienced in this way, but so can fairies and cartoon characters.

---

11. Text on a piece of unpublished art, by Bob Haverluck, seen at the Mennonite Heritage Centre Gallery in the show, "The Secret Treaty between humans and ducks, trees, rivers, bears, and the air and . . .", April 3–June 6, 2009. Permission to quote granted by author.

Fowler's contemporary, Jean Piaget, who influenced educational practices for a long period of time, did not consider pre-rational children capable of faith. However, experts in child theology and spirituality for the last twenty years have come to agree with Fowler's assessment: the capacity for faith is innate.

When my granddaughter, Beatrice, was twenty months old, she loved looking out of her parent's second story bedroom window to watch the birds and squirrels in the tall elm trees lining the street. I'll never forget her awe when she first became aware of the size of one of those majestic elms. She looked down to the grass and then up, and up, and up at the big tree. Filled with wonder and using her emerging words for an expression of praise, she said, "Wow!"

Betty Shannon Cloyd recalls a similar incident with her fifteen month old grandson, Samuel, who whispered a similar "wow!" as he watched a squirrel run up a tree.[12] Infants and young children lack the vocabulary to share their sense of astonishment, but occasionally we are given verbal windows into that lively spiritual space.

Imagine or remember holding a contented infant in your arms. Reflect on the awesome mystery of the gift of new life with which God entrusts us. Now add a few months to the child you are holding. Notice that child's amazement as he or she discovers the world and begins to verbalize the experience.

What other characteristics of primal faith are illustrated by this imagined child or an infant grandchild of your own? If you have such a young grandchild, jot down your observations in a memory journal so you can share them as she or he gets older.

---

12. Betty Shannon Cloyd, *Parents and Grandparents as Spiritual Guides* (Nashville: Upper Room Books, 2000), 101.

As we rediscover the world with infants and toddlers, they bring out our inner playmates and renew our ability to wonder. As infants and toddlers discover the world with their parents, extended family, and the church community, they absorb a specific context for faith. They experience the love of God through their caregivers. Our responsiveness to their expressions and needs builds their trust toward God and their caregivers. The vocabulary with which we surround them provides descriptive tools for their experiences, including their innate consciousness of the divine. As language skills develop and as we introduce spiritual practices such as singing and praying, they gain tools for interacting with the world around them. Infants and toddlers, who often inspire us with the trusting way they depend on our care, bring out the caregiver in us.

Children will not distinguish well between reality and fantasy until the age of seven or so. This is the age where "kids say and do the darndest things."[13] The anecdotes about Sonya, Beatrice, and Samuel give testimony to the innate reality of primal faith.

Stage 1: Intuitive-Projective Faith. By the time children are four to five years of age, the key characteristics describing their faith have evolved:

- They have an intuitive trust and awareness of God's intimate presence.
- They learn the vocabulary and basic habits of faith through imitation.
- They express their faith with the words they hear in their homes and congregations.

---

13. This expression is drawn from the CBS radio show feature, "Kids Say the Darndest Things," hosted by Art Linkletter, airing from the mid 1940s to the late 1960s.

- They relate to images of God as a miracle worker, as baby Jesus, and as angelic.
- They distinguish between fantasy and reality with difficulty.

As a five-year-old preschooler, my granddaughter, Grace, tried to stretch out her bedtime conversation for as long as possible. She asked me, her *Omi*, if I was born in the olden days. "Yes, I was," I answered.

That made sense to Grace. After all, she told me, her dad was old and he came out of Omi's tummy a long time ago. After a reflective silence, Grace added, "That's like Jesus. He came out of God's tummy a long time ago, too."

This was no time for a lesson on the Trinity; this was a chance to delight in the way Grace's young mind made comparisons between the mysterious realities she understood—that her father had been a baby—and the mystery of God becoming flesh in Jesus. To use Fowler's approach, Grace was projecting what she understood about her father and her Omi to try and make sense of the relationship between God the Father and Jesus. Her faith remained strongly intuitive, but she layered her understanding of family onto her emerging idea of how Jesus and God are in relationship.

Four-year-old Eden became my friend when I stayed in her home for two nights. Eden wanted me to read her a bedtime Bible story and help get her ready for sleep. In the process I introduced her to the glad-sad-sorry prayer ritual. Through this prayer, we reflected on the day's highlights and lowlights, wondered if there were things Eden or I needed to say "sorry" for. We named others who needed God's help. The ritual ended with the Aaronic blessing,

"The Lord bless you and keep you, make his face shine on you and give you peace."[14] Then I traced the shape of the cross on Eden's forehead and spoke the words, "In the name of the Father, the Son, and the Holy Spirit. Amen." I concluded by giving her a kiss on that same spot.

Eden took to this ritual immediately, and proceeded to use it with her stuffed animals and dolls in the coming weeks. She learned the vocabulary and practices of faith through imitation. The fluid line between her fantasy life with her toys and what adults refer to as "reality," provided her with an opportunity to lead a simplified form of evening prayer known as *consciousness examen*.[15]

Stage 2: Mythic-Literal Faith. The faith life of most six- to eight-year-old children tends to be expressed through another set of key characteristics:

- They learn and memorize easily.
- They need freedom to express emerging beliefs.
- They often think about Jesus in super-hero terms.
- They often love biblical stories about the weak conquering the strong.
- They identify with favourite Bible characters.
- They enjoy participating in worship, singing, and belonging to the community.

---

14. Paraphrased from Numbers 6: 24-26.

15. The *consciousness examen* is an ancient form of prayer in which one reviews the day in the presence of God, acknowledging those things for which one is grateful, laments, and requests forgiveness. With younger children this can easily be adapted as a "glad, sad, sorry" chat with each other and God.

- They identify strongly with the faith community of their family.

During the last year that I taught grade three, I had my students keep prayer journals.[16] Their prayers illustrated their growing ability to articulate, identify with, and project the faith of their community. Reflect on a few of their prayers as you think about faith at this stage:

> God, please help me be nice today and stay awake.

> Dear God, you are the most powerful Lord.
> You created humans and animals from a tiny mouse to a blue whale. I love you.

> Dear God,
> Thank you for sending your son to us on earth and thank-you for your son dying on the cross to save us from our sins. Thank-you that you helped the Israelites win the battle against Rome. And thank-you that you did not give in to the devil's temptation of revenge and hatred and went on loving them even when they did things they knew they shouldn't do. And I am glad that some of those people who crucified him turned back to loving you and those priests went back to you. Amen.

From early preschool attempts to understand and talk about their faith, children progress in their

---

16. My students had a choice of showing their prayers to me or keeping their prayers between themselves and God. At the end of the year, eight children selected a prayer to give to me for eventual publication in my new work for the broader church, which became *Forming Faith: Prayer Journeys with Children* (Winnipeg: Mennonite Church Canada, 2009), www.mennonitechurch.ca/tiny/1133.

ability to think logically. They start to separate reality from make-believe and truth from lies. They begin to consider the perspectives of others.

For thousands of years, the age of reason has been recognized in children at about the age of seven. As children learn to reason, they start to understand that sin is more than doing things that get them into trouble. It includes attitudes and actions that make it harder to connect with God.

Mythic-literal faith is already filled with many similarities to adult faith, because it readily accepts the ideas of loved and trusted caregivers. It sounds and is experienced as deeply owned, but it will face challenges as children establish critical thinking skills and grow independent of their caregivers.

Many children feel deeply connected to all of God's creation at this stage. They do well at caring for pets and plants. What a great opportunity for grandparents to include them in activities such as planting a garden and marvelling together at the miracle of growth! At this stage, children also love stories of animals with human qualities such as the Berenstain Bears books, to name but one popular example. Many of these stories provide opportunities to talk about good behaviour choices or to develop a commitment to creation care.

At six to eight years of age, children's passion for the created world provides an excellent opportunity for grandparents to help them learn and practice the ethical aspects of following Jesus. So do Bible stories of faith heroes. If children in this stage are regularly acquainted with the stories of Bible characters, they often develop a deep affinity with some of them. When Sonya was at this stage she became very fond of Queen Esther. Several years later, we still include references to Esther when we talk about wisdom, beauty, and courage.

Stage 3: Synthetic-Conventional Faith. For nine- to twelve-year-old children who are approaching adolescence, new factors shape their faith lives:

- They are growing in their awareness of others.
- They question and respond to perceived unfairness.
- They participate in congregational mission and service projects creatively and enthusiastically.
- They welcome involvement in worship leadership roles as ushers, readers, singers, etc.
- They describe their own belief in ways that are similar to those of their faith community.
- They analyze and synthesize the beliefs of their community.
- They respond to God as Creator and Jesus as friend in deeply personal ways.

In the fall of 2010, while the news media covered a devastating flood in Pakistan, several grade six girls from Winnipeg's Home Street Mennonite Church initiated a fund raising campaign. They sent out emails inviting their peers to bake cookies and then sold them to their congregation after worship for several Sundays. The youth pastor provided encouragement and helped out with a few logistics, but the project was a direct expression of the faith of these pre-adolescent girls. Encouragement from the local faith community nurtured their faith, and the project provided some relief resources for a needy corner of God's earth.

During upper elementary and middle school years, the rational mind develops. Children are usually interested in learning about the wider world in which they live. If grandparents are healthy enough, this is the golden age for taking grandchildren on vacations that broaden horizons through museum visits and guided tours. My husband and I have found that our grandchildren are better behaved when they get to be our guests without their parents.

We can expect children between nine and twelve years of age to accept, understand, and synthesize the faith of parents, grandparents, and trusted teachers. When I asked children this age in my congregation where they learned the most about God, they answered unanimously that it was from our pulpit!

As children continue to mature, they begin to explore their faith through the lens of critical thinking and the bigger questions of life that arise. This critical examination helps them move beyond an acceptance of inherited faith toward claiming a faith of their own. When those questions are engaged in upper elementary or middle school, their faith grows in its awareness of others. This inspires many children to take part in group projects where they can energetically advocate on behalf of larger social issues.

The need to explore and examine faith with a critical eye becomes more important as society becomes more secular. Because today's society prizes rationalism, children's natural creativity can be repressed.[17] Dynamic club leaders and teachers, and family service projects help them counteract that trend, grow in faith, and develop the creative skills they need to stand up for the underprivileged. If you are one of those seniors who participates in local service and outreach ministries, take your

---

17. For an interesting reflection by David Csinos on how our educational system tends to squelch creativity in children see http://suchasthese.wordpress.com/2010/08/26/educating-out-of-spirituality/.

grandchildren with you now and then. It is a golden opportunity to help adolescent faith deepen and mature.

If faith is encouraged, and inherited faith, values, and ideas are synthesized after being analyzed, children may claim them as their own. Synthetic-conventional faith continues to mature. In fact, many people who grow up and stay in closely knit Christian communities will remain in this stage for much of their lives—until they spiritually integrate life crises as mature adults.

Stage 4a: Towards an Individuative-Reflective Faith. The next stage of faith development correlates with the duration of adolescence, which can last for a lengthy period of time these days. Today's society encourages young people to explore all of their options and may require them to take more and longer periods of training than we needed. As a result, they settle down with families, careers, and other long-term responsibilities at a much later date than we did. Some sociologists claim that adolescence now lasts until thirty years of age instead of sixteen or even eighteen, as was the case until the 1960s. For that reason, there are levels of progression through Stage 4—"4a," which is discussed here, and "4b," which will be examined in the following chapter.

As children approach adolescence, their physical, emotional, mental, and spiritual lives intertwine on a rollercoaster of change. Children enter puberty at a wide range of ages, but broadly speaking, at roughly thirteen years of age they begin to exhibit certain characteristics:

- They critique, question, and claim faith and belief systems.

- They value belonging to their church community above belief or behaviour codes.
- They articulate their own beliefs and examine other faith traditions.
- They use thinking that confirms their gut feelings to make well ordered faith decisions.
- They often relate to Jesus as confidante, guide, and counsellor.
- They desire friendships in which they can test the values, faith, and beliefs that have formed them.
- They look for those who "walk the talk."
- They keenly detect and resent adults who are not truthful with them.
- They often work enthusiastically as service workers in places such as church camps or on mission trips.
- They bless us with testimonies, questions, insights, skills, and emerging leadership.

A student at a private high school in Warrington, Florida, wrote the following prayer, which illustrates how he relates to Jesus as confidante, guide, and counsellor:

> Lord, give me your courage, for I cannot stand
> up against the forces that strike my soul.
> Give me your will, so that I can use the gifts
> that you have given me confidently and wisely,
> every day of my life.
> Give me your love, so I can break through the
> shackles of my hatred and live in love and peace.
> Give me your faith, for I doubt the almighty
> when things go wrong.
> Lord, help me to live as you did. Amen.[18]

18. Sam Tatel, an untitled prayer in *Life Can Be a Wild Ride*, ed. Marilyn Kielbasa (Winona: St. Mary's Press, 2001), 96.

Cognitively, adolescents have the relatively new skill of being able to imagine what others think. They notice, question, and compare the different worldviews of their church, school, and virtual communities. No doubt your mind will fill rapidly with anecdotes about this tendency!

Because adolescents *need* to figure out what they think and believe in relation to what *others* think and believe, they tend to be preoccupied with themselves. Experiencing this stage is essential for the adolescent to progress to an owned—or individuated—set of beliefs and values.

Today's world is also more secular and diverse than the "officially" Christian culture in which the boomer generation matured. This presents many obstacles for people whose faith is not thoroughly individuated. As the introduction outlined, many of the young people we know and love live in settings that are much more culturally diverse than the ones we knew as youth. This more diverse context involves them in repeated examination and defence of their values and belief systems—and over a much longer period of time than was the norm for us. If the young people who are dear to you fall into this category, being a good and loving listener is critical, even when you'd much rather give advice and answers.

Additionally, today's children and youth are part of the "iGeneration," with digital tools at their fingertips. They connect with a wide range of communities that offer competing sets of values. It is likely that their conventional faith will face challenges we never experienced. As they face and integrate these challenges spiritually, they will examine conventional faith more critically. They may progress to a more strongly personalized or individuated faith. When this more individuated faith develops alongside a personal relationship with God—in which they feel themselves to be deeply known and loved by God and the church community—the adolescent forms a solid set of beliefs, values, and commitments. This foundation prepares the way for baptism and membership in the church.

There is great reluctance among many of today's youth and young adults to step forward, articulate their faith, and make baptismal commitments. Even seminary students I have interviewed are shy about praying aloud; they aren't sure that church is a safe place to expose their spiritual reality. They fear being rejected because their faith won't sound traditional enough. This is a clear example of placing value on belonging over belief or behaviour.

Seniors have a unique opportunity to encourage and mentor youth toward confessing their faith and preparing for baptism; they are not the generation from whom the youth are individuating or claiming their independence. With God's grace and wisdom, seniors can often build relationships of integrity and trust with youth. They provide safe places for youth to air their doubts and test their emerging, personally owned faith. With prayerful discernment, seniors can use the strength of those relationships to speak the right words at the right time.

Conclusion

Understanding each phase of a grandchild's development can go a long way toward knowing how to encourage them on their faith journey. As we reflect on the gifts and nature of children's faith and normal developmental patterns, the puzzling aspects of our children's and grandchildren's lives will fit into the broader context of how faith changes in the developmental stages of life. Perhaps that will bring comfort when, or if, we feel that our families have failed the younger generations.

We live in rapidly changing circumstances that bring confusion along with new opportunities. However, it is good to remember that the Holy Spirit is known to be particularly active in periods of rapid change. Consider the history of the early church, of Protestant denominations during the Reformation, the Great Revival during a tumultuous era of American development, or of the emergence of the Pentecostal movement during the wild years of the early twentieth century. These periods are rich with stories about the movement of the Holy Spirit in people's lives. Coming generations may well look back at our time in a similar way.

It is also good to note once more that the general faith growth guidelines described here will not describe each person's spiritual journey. Spiritual growth remains a dance between predictable maturation and unpredictable encounters of the Holy.

Reflection and Discussion Questions

Children are members of God's family

1. In what ways have you experienced the church providing good "lap experiences" for its children?

2. What expressions of faith and wonder by a child have added sparkle and vitality to the spiritual life of your family or congregation?

3. How have your thoughts about guilt, truth, and children's innocence influenced your expectations of the children in your life to tell the truth and accept responsibility for their actions?

4. Thinking about God in terms of playing hide and seek seems unusually playful for mature adults. In what ways can such reflection enrich our thoughts and feelings about God?

5. If children possess a spiritual awareness from infancy on, what is it that keeps us from taking their faith seriously?

Primal Faith

1. Describe and share any experiences with young children that came to mind as you read about this early stage of faith.

2. If a young child in your life is not receiving the foundation for a trusting and loving relationship with God, what are some ways you can help build that foundation in their lives?

3. If the blending of fantasy and reality in the young troubles you, what are some constructive ways of encouraging children's faith that honour their way of engaging with life?

4. How have children blessed and encouraged you through their expressions of primal faith?

Intuitive-Projective Faith

1. Describe and share the experiences with preschool children that came to mind as you read about this stage of faith.

2. When preschool children make statements that do not match our understanding of God or otherwise ring true, how can we bless their present level of insight and still encourage their growth?

3. What opportunities do the young people in your lives have to learn and practice Christian vocabulary and practices? Are there some grace-filled ways you can increase those opportunities?

4. How have the gifts of children at this stage blessed and encouraged you?

Mythic-Literal Faith

1. Describe and share the experiences with children in primary school that came to mind as you read about this stage of faith.
2. How do you understand the difference between faith that expresses, identifies with, and projects the faith of their community; and more mature, conventional faith?
3. In your family system and your congregation, what opportunities exist for seniors and primary age children to talk about faith and belief? Can you imagine and promote some new ways of encouraging this dialogue?
4. How have the gifts of children at this stage blessed and encouraged you?

Synthetic-Conventional Faith

1. Describe and share the experiences with pre-adolescent children that came to mind as you read about this stage of faith.
2. How can you help children in this phase of life respond to Jesus' instructions to care for the underprivileged as an expression of faith?
3. Critical thinking is so necessary for preadolescent growth toward an owned faith. How can you help children you know deal with the challenges that arise as they engage in critical thinking?
4. How have the gifts of children at this stage blessed and encouraged you?

Individuative-Reflective Faith

1. What stories of youth in this critical testing stage can you share with each other to increase

your understanding of this part of the faith journey?

2. If you shared the "river-story" activity in Chapter Two with youth who are dear to you, how might the process start conversations that would build trust and help them share their faith with you?

3. What stories of apparent or real rejection by dear people of this age do you need to offer to God in lament?

4. How is your life blessed by people at this age and stage of the journey of faith?

4

How Does Faith Mature?

As adolescents become young adults, some aspects of earlier faith development stages linger. Some characteristics of the later stages described in this chapter may have surfaced when they were younger. It is clear that faith does not develop and mature in the same way for each person. Nevertheless, Fowler's classic description of faith stages remains a solid guide for thinking and talking about the journey toward maturity in Christ.

From an early sensory awareness of the divine and a foundation of being loved and accepted, Christians begin to project their intuited sense of God onto the world they experience. The merged worlds of fantasy and reality encountered by young children are gradually identified and separated. By synthesizing these understandings with broader life experience, and with the faith passed on by Christian mentors, they move from literal to deeper understandings of the righteousness, love, and wisdom of God. And then, if they claim it, the faith becomes their own. They journey on from that point as Christian adults who continue to reflect on their faith and grow toward Christian maturity.

Progressing toward Christian Maturity

As mentioned in Chapter Three, individuals often remain in the fourth stage of faith development for a significant period of time. For that reason, there are levels of progression through it—from "4a," which was explored previously, and "4b," which we will look at here.

Stage 4b: Individuative-Reflective Faith. Whether or not young adults have fully entered Stage 4b, and whether or not they consider themselves Christian, certain characteristics are likely to be part of their faith journey as they move forward:

- They will critique the attitudes and values of institutions and older adults.
- They will commit themselves to life partners and directions.
- They learn to live courageously with uncertainty.
- They seek authenticity in self and others.
- They need to articulate questions, but don't necessarily want answers.
- They become increasingly independent in both thought and action.
- They value mutual, interpersonal perspectives.
- They recognize the impact of social and legal systems.
- They need to be heard for who they *are*, not for whom they represent.
- They use cynicism as part of growth.

This is the phase where people leave home emotionally and often geographically, and it is quite common among young adults and those who are in their thirties. They look critically at the assumptions of their home and faith communities, and those of the social class of which they are a part. Aspects of this stage will recur whenever adults face a major life crisis.

In a post-Christian context, this is the time when many feel freed to leave the church in which they were raised, to determine just who they want to be and what they will believe as adults. This individuation can be very painful for their families. It is especially so when young adults cling to new value and belief systems that they have not evaluated as critically as they have evaluated the systems from which they are claiming their independence.

According to Fowler, to move through this stage one must stop depending on others and shape one's own set of values in a full awareness of one's surrounding social systems and institutions.[1] This process includes testing ideas and naming doubt. Articulating reflections on such a process may be limited to the academically inclined. Those who prefer a more hands-on approach will find other ways to separate themselves from inherited faith as they claim something "new" for their own.

Transition into this stage is often triggered by a crisis or a sense that previously accepted beliefs are inadequate to face the trials of life. This stage can involve major struggle. Although it may be difficult, this is a stage where powerful concepts are developed and owned, where logic is highly valued and cultivated. Those who stay in the church also face these questions and doubts, but they can find

---

1. James W. Fowler, *Weaving the New Creation: Stages of Faith and the Public Church* (San Francisco: HarperSanFrancisco, 1991), 109.

good ways of connecting with faith and the life of the church through a variety of spiritual practices.

Faith of the Saints: Faith Tested

The following two phases of faith, the fifth and sixth stages—the conjunctive and universalizing faith as described by Fowler—are less common than the preceding ones. They represent the ideal of maturation, generally developing through growth in times of crisis that plunge people into deep doubt. If you have been spared such crises, your faith may still grow mature and deep without experiencing Stages 5 and 6.

Some people enter into such times of crisis voluntarily. Mature adult faith can be developed through experiences like those described in the following report from a member of Christian Peacemaker Teams (CPT). This particular CPTer was on a voluntary assignment in Hebron, Palestine. His assignment was to accompany Palestinian children as they crossed through a trailer checkpoint on their way to school. Children as young as six years of age had to pass under metal detectors, have their bags checked by soldiers, and were sometimes patted down. The presence of CPTers reduced the harassment children faced.

Tarek Abuata, a Palestine Project support coordinator writes:

> One day after my friend and I finished patrolling for an hour, absolutely exhausted, we ran into a settler who spit in our faces, and called us Nazis for helping these terrorist children. Do you think I thought, "it takes love to fight an Occupation?" No, no! At that moment I said to myself, "I would like to slap him!"
>
> A few days later, six five-year-old Palestinian children were detained by six Israeli soldiers for playing with toy guns on Eid. (Eid is the

celebration that ends the Ramadan fast.) Looking at the scene I actually softened. I stood back wondering which kids are being abused more, those five-year-olds with toy guns or those eighteen-year-olds with real guns. I could only feel compassion for all involved, including myself.

On several occasions I've experienced getting beaten by Israeli soldiers, and I've experienced the ugliness of the Israeli Occupation on a very deep level. As a privileged Palestinian, I know that I have truly experienced only 30 percent of what other Palestinians my age living in Palestine experience. Nevertheless, I know that more love works . . . I know that more love works because I have experienced both settlers and Israeli soldiers who were transformed through the love energy we faced their hatred with . . . I look into a soldier's eyes directly for him to see my soul through my eyes, and in the process, he sees his own soul through that mirror, connecting us at a profound level that can't be verbalized, and waking us both out of our societal self-inflicted nightmares.[2]

Stage 5: Conjunctive Faith. Fowler uses the term, "conjunctive" for Stage 5 because many aspects of life are brought together like a conjunction joins ideas in a sentence. Those who are experiencing conjunctive faith will exhibit several characteristics:

- They long for insights into a fuller understanding of God and God's activity in the world.

---

2. Christian Peacemaker Teams electronic bulletin, December 21, 2011, CPT Net archives. http://www.cpt.org/cptnet/2011/12/14/palestine-letter-it-takes-love-fight-occupation%E2%80%9D.

- They participate actively in the mission of the church.
- They dialogue with other denominations and faith traditions from a position of rootedness within one's own.
- They are able to connect with a group without sacrificing their individuality.[3]

Adults who have made it through the individuation and thought-filled reflection of Stage 4b may come to realize that the logic and concepts of that stage are not adequate for responding to the complexities of life. This realization can push them toward a more layered approach to faith, truth, and life as strands of understanding come together.[4]

In this stage, people become capable of deeper dialogue with those of other faiths. They grow in their ability to live with paradoxes and ambiguities. They learn to reconcile the impact of the conscious and unconscious their lives. As veterans of critical reflection, people on this stage of the faith journey may develop a new appreciation for symbols and rituals that bring deeper understandings to their realities. This stage often develops as individuals reclaim and rework their past, and learn to listen to deeper voices within.

Stage 6: Universalizing Faith. Those who grow to maturity in Christ may come to exhibit another set of characteristics in their life of faith:

---

3. Summarized from Robert J. Keeley, "Faith Development and Faith Formation: More than Just Ages and Stages," *Lifelong Faith* 4, no. 3 (2010): 20–27.

4. Fowler, *Weaving the New Creation*, 111.

- They have a continuing expansion of faith that welcomes new challenges.
- They grow in faith as they remain open to the Holy Spirit's reminders of Jesus' presence in and around us and others, including our grandchildren.
- They observe carefully and share God's care for all of creation.
- They rejoice to participate in what God is doing.
- They live with an increasing sense of yieldedness to the purposes of God.
- They grow in their trust that Jesus is always with us and in their abilities to let go and depend on God the Father, Son, and Holy Spirit, to sustain and guide them, regardless of the situation.

While the conjunctive stage of faith was able to hold many different aspects of faith and belief in dialogue, those who reach the universalizing stage "are grounded in oneness with the power of being or God."[5] They devote themselves to love and justice as they trust and lean into the future of God. They identify fully with God's perspective, rather than one that is personally motivated or defined by numerous outside influences.

When we are with these people, we get a glimpse of God's dream for what humans are meant to be: in full communion with God. They live out their faith with radical abandon. Although many of us may struggle to reach this stage on this side of heaven, adults and seniors who tend their spirituality may find glimmers of its emergence.

---

5. Ibid., 113.

There are a few retired church leaders in my congregation who exhibit many aspects of this universalizing faith. They engage younger leaders with an inspiring, gracious humility that truly reflects the art of spiritual grandparenting. One continues a ministry of healing prayer in her home, but is reluctant to talk about it. Another provides interim pastoral ministry in other congregations as the need arises. A third continues to lead mid-week Bible studies, where he shares from his life as a respected Bible scholar.

These senior mentors are genuinely interested in others' welfare. They exude a gentleness that draws younger people to them for advice. However, they give that advice only after they have assured their young friends that each will recognize what is best in their own situation.

Other theologians are adding to Fowler's categories describing the adult faith journey. For instance, Brian McLaren suggests that adults live through repeated cycles of experiencing faith. A view through a lens of simplicity is followed by recognition of greater complexity, which can lead to a time of perplexity that is finally resolved in a stage of harmony.[6] Adults who are spared the challenges of perplexity may find their spiritual lives revolve through cycles of simplicity and complexity.

---

6. Brian McLaren's book *Naked Spirituality: A Life with God in 12 Simple Words* (New York: HarperOne, 2011), characterises the adult faith journey though these descriptors. A *Publisher's Weekly* review shared on McLaren's website describes his book as follows, "Conventional Christians may not welcome McLaren's extravagant invitation to those on the religious margins, but anyone wanting to conserve the spiritual spark in themselves or someone else will find this book a gentle and generous tract" (http://brianmclaren.net/archives/books/brians-books/naked-spirituality-a-life-with-g-1.html).

In addition, whether child or adult, it is important to remember that we have different styles of spirituality. We seek to know God through approaches that center on words, emotions, symbols, and actions that appeal to us.[7] Each person's unique blend of spiritual styles will impact how, but not if, that person's faith matures.

What about Conversion?

Conversion is a natural part of faith development. It results from an encounter with the Holy Spirit in which we become acutely aware of, and say yes, to God. This encounter is generally linked to a growing awareness of the problem and lure of evil and a sense of responsibility for one's own choices.

What is the right age for conversion? Children can certainly respond holistically to the activity of the Holy Spirit in their lives. When they do, we affirm and encourage their encounters, giving thanks and glory to God for these gifts of his presence. Some children make deep and life changing commitments long before adulthood, which stay with them and are affirmed as they mature.

However, these experiences are different from adult conversion. For adults, conversion involves a reorientation and a grateful submission to God as the center of one's life. It leads to believers baptism in Anabaptist churches, or to the mature

---

7. The publications of Corinne Ware, David Csinos, Joyce Bellous, and Urban T. Holmes use words, emotions, symbols, and actions to illustrate our different ways of knowing God. In addition, Bellous, Csinos, and Denise Peltomaki, a former children's pastor, have developed self-assessment approaches for children and adults that utilize these tools. They are available from Tall Pine Press at www.tallpinepress.com.

rededication of one's life in churches that celebrate infant baptism.

As children and youth respond to their age-appropriate sense of the Holy and learn the stories of God, the image of God within them blossoms. Maturation and faith-nurture generally prepare the way for conversion. As Christian educator Catherine Stonehouse states, "the time must come when persons choose God as the center of life."[8]

The process of saying "yes" to God will continue throughout life on the journey of faith, but just as the decision to marry marks a watershed in the relationship between a man and a woman, choosing God as the center of life marks a watershed of conversion. It points the way to mature commitment and adult faith. This faith will continue to evolve throughout life's journey. If nurtured, it will deepen. Christ will increasingly be formed within the adult.

James Fowler describes a free spirited dance between faith development based on stages of maturity and personal interaction with the Holy Spirit. The Holy Spirit's work resists classification. It is active as God among us and in us at all stages of the spiritual journey. At times, the Holy Spirit is evident as an awareness of God believing in us. The cover of the 2004 NOOMA DVD, *Dust*, describes this concept:

> "Believing in God is important, but what about God believing in us? . . . It's easy for us to sometimes get down on ourselves. To feel "not good enough" or feel like we don't have what it takes. By referring to the disciples Jesus chose as evidence that we can be very fallible human

---

8. Catherine Stonehouse, *Joining Children on the Spiritual Journey: Nurturing a Life of Faith* (Grand Rapids: Baker Academic, 1998), 167.

beings and still receive the invitation to partner with God in living toward heaven on earth, *Dust* makes the point that God does believe in us."[9]

If an adolescent or teen encounters this experience of the Holy during the rollercoaster of identity formation we refer to as youth, it may lead to a life-transforming conversion experience.

Conversion can happen in dramatic or gentle and gradual ways. The important test of conversion is growth as a follower of Jesus. After conversion, the journey toward maturity in faith must continue as it faces new trials, new sets of doubts, and new experiences of grace, thus reaching new levels of wisdom and commitment.

An adulthood entry into faith development can be more abrupt. Sara Miles, an organizer and a completely secular journalist who covered revolutionary wars in the 1980s, encountered Christ and the church as a mature adult. Sara described her rapid maturing of faith by comparing it to the ways she had responded to the revolution. "I learn[ed] that it's possible to fall in love with a revolution—then doubt it, fight with it, lose faith in it, and return with a sense of humour and a harder lasting love. I would have to learn the same thing about church when I was much older, and it would be no easier."[10]

Falling in love with faith, doubting it, fighting with it, and losing it, only to return to it with a sense of humour and a harder, lasting love, has many similarities to Fowler's descriptions of the faith stages of adults.

---

9. Rob Bell, *Dust*, NOOMA DVD (Grandville: Flannel, 2004).

10. Sara Miles, *Take this Bread* (New York: Ballantine Books, 2007), 35.

When Young People Choose to Reject Christian Faith or the Church

Do you lament the dear young people—or adults— in your life who are not growing in faith the way Fowler's stages suggest, or the way you think they should? Are they getting stuck along the road to love and wisdom? Some people do get trapped along the way. They enter adulthood with a shallow faith that is inadequate to meet the challenges of following Christ as an adult.[11] And sometimes they reject the faith that is dear to you.

If Christian faith is to be freely chosen, we must also accept that it can be freely rejected. The very idea is troubling, uncomfortable, and even painful to name in the company of other Christians. Perhaps that is why the subject of faith denial doesn't get enough attention. Yet, when I mention that it is an issue in my own family during speaking engagements or seminars, attention is clearly piqued. I hear from grateful older adults who worry about the faith lives of their adult children or grandchildren, and from younger adults who often feel misunderstood for the way they seek meaning and purpose in life.

As society becomes more secular and Christianity becomes less mainstream, many of the social reasons for belonging to a church community have disappeared. And as our children live increasingly "plugged in" lives through social networking and

---

11. Kenda Creasy Dean, *Almost Christian: What the Faith of Our Teenagers is Telling the American Church* (New York: Oxford University Press, 2010). Creasy Dean writes clearly about the multi-generational problem of people who develop a feel-good, self-centered faith, but never progress toward the mature or "thick faith" that orients itself around the church's activity in God's mission.

electronic browsing, their virtual electronic community replaces family and church community as a major source of identity formation.

An increasing number of our children and grandchildren choose against baptism into the congregational community. Even among those who do get baptized, many soon disappear from organized congregational life. Those who stay in our congregations may find their pastoral care among trusted peers in a "safe place," such as a coffee shop or a library, rather than in their family home or church building. This is our current social reality. It has a major impact on the spiritual journeys of our children, our grandchildren, and on congregational health.

How do we understand these dear ones who grew up in the faith, but reject the church and remain in a testing or rejecting stage? More importantly, how do we affirm the ongoing work of God's Spirit in their lives?

Margaret is an older Russian Mennonite woman with a large, diverse, and blended family. Only one family unit from her clan attends church. She describes her situation from a hopeful perspective:

> Now, how crazy is this? We grew up in a firm Christian home with parents who experienced the hell of the Russian Revolution, displacement in a strange unknown country, and eked out a living under severe circumstances, while their relatives who stayed behind survived the onslaughts of a system that wanted to take away their faith. Now we have a generation that isn't sure that all this has enough credibility for them to embrace the faith. Go figure! But as I work through my thinking on the subject, I'm convinced they have a faith . . . [which] they

express in the quality of the choices they make
in their lives.[12]

Although Margaret laments, she has found ways
of seeing God at work in her children's and grandchildren's lives. She finds these words of Colossians
1:16-17 helpful, "All things have been created
through him and for him . . . [and] in whom all
things hold together." It gives her great comfort to
claim Jesus as the center and the end of the journeys that all of her family members are travelling,
whether they recognize it or not. She also finds comfort in remembering that the breath God breathed
into Adam is within us still, transferred into every
child at birth. Believing that we are all filled with
God's breath reaffirms her belief in the worth of
each human, and of God's presence in each member
of her diverse and largely secular clan.

We may not all share Margaret's perspective.
However, it is important to remember that when
youth and young adults who are dear to us reject
our beliefs or values, it is critical to remain in good
relationship with them—whether they return to our
faith or not. We must affirm whatever we can. By
assuring them that our acceptance of them does not
depend upon their confession of faith or regular
church attendance, we encourage them to remain
part of our families and communities.

It may help us to remember that Christian life is
a matter of believing, behaving, and belonging.[13] We

12. This quote is taken from email correspondence with
Margaret Heese of Swift Current, Saskatchewan, with her
permission.

13. The idea of faith as a matter of behaving, believing, and
belonging is quite common among church historians who
reflect on the changing priority of these three aspects of faith

have sometimes focused on believing to the detriment of the faith forming power of belonging and behaving. The value of belonging to a family or a church community during our current period of social change and upheaval is not to be underestimated. Today's young adults repeatedly name the strength of its influence on their lives. During interviews with students at Associated Mennonite Biblical Seminary in the fall of 2010, I learned that many of them avoid sharing deep questions and scepticism about faith with their own congregations. They fear losing the acceptance of their church communities.

Scepticism about faith may be a tool for continued critical reflection and growth. Sometimes a rejection of the Christian faith is also a prophetic indictment toward the lack of authenticity sensed, rightly or wrongly so, in our expressions of that faith. Such an indictment can be threatening. It is a struggle to not take the rejection of our beliefs personally, and to maintain a good relationship with those who are critical, but it is worth the effort.

Such criticisms encourage us to look more closely at exactly *what* is being critiqued. Is the faith they are rejecting actually *our* faith? Detractors may be reacting to misrepresentations of Christianity by various groups. The New Atheist movement[14], for

---

at different times in church history. Some, such as Phyllis Tickle, suggest we are moving into an era where belonging will be more important than believing.

14. To familiarize yourself with New Atheism, do a web search of the spokesmen for the movement, Sam Harris, Lucas C. Dennett, Richard Dawkins, Victor J. Stenger, and the late Christopher Hitchens. For a more positive summary of this worldview, browse the website of a social movement called "Brights" http://the-brights.net/ promoting a naturalistic worldview rather than focusing on the negation of a supernatural religious perspective.

example, spends considerable effort pitting science against religion, debunking faith as myth and super-stition.[15] This twenty-first-century movement is strongly shaped by "enlightenment thinking" with its praise of reason and strong reactions to what it perceives to be the political and social abuse of religion in North America. It seeks to actively counter, criticize, and explain the influence of religion by rational argument.

How are Christians responding to these critiques? Numerous debates in bookstores and online seek to prove Christianity right through Apologetics, the science of focussing on the flaws of other world-views. If you appreciate satire, Becky Garrison's book, *The New Atheist Crusaders and Their Unholy Grail*,[16] provides an easy-to-read critique from a religious satirist who is also a contributing writer for *Sojourners*[17] magazine.

Whatever alternative set of beliefs and values to which our beloved young people ascribe, we need to stay in touch with them. We must spend the time

---

15. New Atheism may be more representative of Canadian youth than American. In the US, some youth pastors contend that the biggest problem among young people who reject the church is moralistic therapeutic deism (MTD), an approach that reduces Christian faith to niceties. See Kenda Creasy Dean's *Almost Christian: What the Faith of Our Teenagers is Telling the American Church* (New York: Oxford University Press, 2010).

16. Becky Garrison, *The New Atheist Crusaders and Their Unholy Grail: The Misguided Quest to Destroy Your Faith* (Nashville: Thomas Nelson, 2007). You can also read Garrison's blog for an introduction to the conversation between socially-minded Christians and New Atheists: www.beckygarrison.com.

17. *Sojourners* magazine explores social justice issues through a biblical lens.

required to find out what is important to them, and why. If they choose to not claim Christian faith, what do they believe? Whose ideas are influencing them? Knowing what they think is important for maintaining respectful relationships.

If we extend respect and continued acceptance, we can also expect to receive it. While it is tough to respond to an outright rejection of our beliefs without becoming defensive, tending our own faith life and living it with humble integrity will help us to stay in healthy relationships with those who have turned away. A judgmental rejection of their views will only destroy the remaining trust in the relationship. God can work in all kinds of circumstances. We must trust that the Holy Spirit is still active in their lives, even though they cannot currently acknowledge God's presence. As we wait and pray for opportunities to speak humbly and personally of our hope and inspiration for life, we can take comfort in Jesus' parable about the father who waits for the return of his son.

I have lived with this reality in my own family. Extended email conversations on theological topics with my son, Lucas, have tested and articulated the core of my convictions, and they have been an important part of maintaining a good relationship with him. It has not been easy, but it has been very good. Email allows us to communicate in a "safe space" on these issues. It gives both of us time to carefully consider what we write before hitting "send," and it hides potential voice tremors that could heighten the intensity of a spoken conversation.

The experience has helped me to live and believe with greater integrity. I have read New Atheist literature to gain a deeper understanding of his ideas and his critique of Christianity. Affirming and thanking

Lucas for acts of truthfulness, justice, compassion, and family loyalty have been an important part of staying in good relationship. I have been blessed to observe how the values that shaped his childhood continue to shape his choices. I find comfort in remembering that faith has aspects of believing, behaving, and belonging to it. Even though belief may not be present at this point, it is only one third of the equation—and the other two thirds are present.

However, after coming to understand each other's perspectives, and realizing that continued discussion brings more pain than gain, I have closed that conversation for now. I love my son unconditionally and focus instead on the many things we share.

What we share includes two precious grandchildren; an infant, Jacob, and Beatrice, a soon to be four-year-old who considers me a favoured playmate. Our divergence of beliefs impacts how my son parents, and how I and my husband grandparent. At this point, Beatrice responds intuitively to my love as "God with skin on," a key characteristic of her primal faith. She likes to play with our Christmas crèche and asks to play with it during ordinary time as well as Advent and Christmas. We pray together before mealtimes and at sleepovers. As we talk and play, my faith is a natural part of the relationship.

However, Beatrice is quickly reaching the age where she will be ready for Bible stories. I don't want to disturb her or our relationship with stories and ideas with which her father will disagree. We've invited her parents into a conversation about her faith nurture. We wait for that conversation and pray it won't become divisive. Our relationship with our children and grandchildren is more precious than any specific story or ritual. We are learning to trust that God's Spirit will continue to work in their lives, even if we can't provide the kind of direct Christian nurture that we'd like to.

Our situation is far from unique. In many congregations, the absence of three and four-generation family units is striking. In my congregation, two former church leaders have told me about grandchildren who identify themselves as New Atheists. Both of these elderly people deliberately keep in touch with their grandchildren by focusing on the things they have in common—like music, ecology, and city politics. They converse with their grandchildren about non-divisive topics as they pray and wait with hope for a time when searching questions about Christianity will arise. They have found that forcing the issue is not profitable; it disrupts the relationship of trust.

Another older acquaintance said that she and her husband used to invite their secular children and grandchildren to participate in social activities with their church friends. It was a way of connecting them with the community of believers. Now that their energy is waning, they can no longer host such large gatherings. To continue connecting meaningfully with their extended families, they often miss church celebrations of holidays like Christmas and Easter. They have learned to appreciate the present, and they live as unapologetic Christians in a fairly secular family community. They love and accept their children and grandchildren as they are.

As we find the courage to name and discuss with other seniors the difficult reality of families who don't share our faith, many more ways of supporting our dear ones on this alternate road to the journey of faith will emerge. I hope these stories have opened that conversation.

Conclusion

The last two chapters introduced a set of tools to help understand and nurture faith. Fowler's faith stages have been tested and found reliable in a general way, but they may not perfectly describe each of us or the young people who are dear to us. As we build good relationships of trust and unconditional acceptance with them, we can adapt the information in these chapters to gain a truer understanding of their unique spiritual journeys.

The sections about more developed faith may remind us of our own journeys toward Christian maturity and provide guideposts for what lies ahead. Perhaps they will encourage and nudge us forward spiritually.

Part of Christian maturity consists of selfless giving of oneself to God's mission. This has a direct relationship to how we perceive our role as grandparents. As we embrace this part of God's mission, we will move from our "God with skin on" roles of relating to infants and toddlers to being gentle guides. Now and then we may even get to be the "sage on the stage," and respond to questions from the young.

The art of spiritually grandparenting young people is a shared ministry between homes and congregations. God has a place and a role for all of us, no matter where we find ourselves on the faith journey. When extended families reclaim their role as faith nurturers, they help the next generations develop their identities as God's people. If it is not possible to connect in this way with your own grandchildren, perhaps God will direct other older Christians their way, just as God may direct you toward a friendly relationship with other young people who would benefit from your attention and affection. This can happen informally or as part of an adopt-a-grandparent program.

Christian seniors are a major resource that an aging church can offer to young families who are nurturing Christian identity and growth in their children. Engaging in the art of spiritual grandparenting provides a humble example of faithful living to others, even those who choose to reject what we believe. That example can have a subtle but powerful influence.

Reflection and Discussion Questions

Stage 4b: Individuative-Reflective Faith

1. Are there young adults in your life who are living through the Individuative-Reflective stage of faith as active participants in the life of the church? If so, share some of their stories here as a complement to the stories shared in the previous section.

2. What aspects of this faith stage have been most predominant in your journey through life crisis of loss and change?

3. Where do you find spaces for safe conversation with those who are living through this stage of life and faith? How can you engage in respectful listening to them, while giving witness to the hope you have in Christ?

4. When are we called to hold doubt and belief, and ambiguity and certainty, in a healthy tension?

Stages 5 and 6: Conjunctive and Universalizing Faith

1. Which descriptions of mature faith resonated most deeply with your own ways of knowing God and relating to God's people?

2. As you read these descriptions of mature faith, which leaders came to mind? Share stories from their lives to help you understand these aspects of the faith journey.

3. What spiritual practices could help you mature in your own faith journey?

4. How can a deeper understanding of the different stages of faith help you relate to the young people who are dear to you?

Conversion

1. What stories of conversion in young people can you share to build deeper understanding of this aspect of growing in faith?

2. Where would you place yourself on a continuum line from belief in conversion as a matter of choice, to belief in conversion as a total act of God's Spirit?

3. Do you agree or disagree with the sentiment described in the NOOMA DVD that "God believes more deeply in us than we believe in God"? What are the implications of this for the way we look for signs of spiritual growth in people who claim a conversion experience?

4. What are your thoughts about the interplay between maturation, faith nurture, and conversion? How spiritually and ethically mature do people need to be to receive believers baptism?

When young people choose to reject Christian faith or the church

1. What stories can you share about young people in your life who have rejected the church or Christian beliefs?

2. What issues make it hardest for young people who have rejected the church to believe or

participate in church life? Are these issues central to the reconciling gospel of Jesus Christ, or are they cultural expressions of it?

3. When does our hospitality toward people who are filled with doubt and disbelief compromise the integrity of our church as a witnessing community?

4. What other aspects of our church life compromise our witness? Can an awareness of these other shortcomings help us extend grace toward those with a different world view?

5

Tapping the Spiritual Potential of Stories and Holiday Celebrations

The blessing that comes with tale-telling is the awareness that we have now done our duty to life. We have distilled our experiences to the point that they can become useful to someone younger.[1]

Sharing Our Stories as Testimony

Stories, holidays, and grandparents belong together. Many holiday gatherings include family stories that shape our identities as they connect the generations with each other. As grandparents or seniors, we have unique access to five generations in our memory banks. We remember and tell stories about our parents and grandparents. We draw on stories from our own lives, as well as from those of our children and grandchildren. Perhaps we've even moved from hosting family gatherings to sitting back and sharing our treasure trove of stories. Sharing glimpses

---

1. Joan Chittister, *The Gift of Years: Growing Older Gracefully* (New York: BlueBridge, 2008), 88. Emphasis mine.

of our experiences provides the opportunity to connect with a bigger story as well—the story of God's people through the ages.

David Csinos recalls a variety of identity-shaping family stories, including this favourite bedtime story of "The Ceiling Stars" that he heard from his mother:

> "When my mother was a girl, the ceiling of her bedroom was painted blue and covered with little gold stars—the kind we used to get in kindergarten for answering questions correctly or picking up after ourselves. Sometimes when she awoke throughout the evening, my mother would look down at her bed and find it blanketed with fallen stars. She would call for my grandmother, who quietly came into her room with a stepladder, placed it near the edge of my mother's bed, climbed to the top step, and glued the fallen starts back onto the ceiling one by one . . . "[2]

Grandparents and stories belong together. "Tell me a story about when Daddy was little" is a common request from my grandchildren. It is a universal request, one that helps children to claim their place in a multigenerational network.

Life stories also help older adults make sense of their place and purpose. As we think and talk about our lives, or begin writing memoirs, we learn to identify how God has been present throughout our life experiences. Can we name the loving gifts of God? Can we see God's grace-filled companionship through the easy and difficult experiences? Where

---

2. David M. Csinos, *Children's Ministry that Fits: Beyond One-Size-Fits-All Approaches to Nurturing Children's Spirituality*, (Eugene: Wipf and Stock, 2011), 108.

has God's Spirit provided the courage we needed to face life's challenges? Sharing our stories as testimony to God's role in our lives leads us from the obvious to the obscure ways that God has been with us.[3] That inspires gratitude.

Whether we are providing a sense of continuity and rootedness for younger people, engaging in nostalgic reminiscence, or reviewing our lives to affirm their religious meaning, stories are important. They are packed with spiritual potential. Reminiscing over the account of our lives helps us to resolve, reorganize, and reintegrate significant accomplishments and defeats.[4] Stories help us define who we are and *whose* we are. They link our individual narratives into a larger social and spiritual network.

Reflecting on his mother's stories, David Csinos agrees. "[Such] stories captured a piece of my innermost being and formed the core of my identity."[5]

As children grow and link together stories about uncles, aunts, cousins, parents, and grandparents, their family identity develops. Our use of Bible narratives plays a similar role. Learning about God's big story and how it extends to include us and the generations still to come helps to shape children's spiritual identity as part of that big family.

---

3. Charles Olsen, *The Wisdom of the Seasons: How the Church Year Helps Us Understand Our Congregational Stories* (Herndon: The Alban Institute, 2009), 68.

4. Janeen Bertsche Johnson, *Reminiscence and the Elderly*, an unpublished independent study paper (Goshen College: Independent Study for Departmental Honors in Psychology, May 1, 1986), 35.

5. David M. Csinos, *Children's Ministry that Fits: Beyond One-Size-Fits-All Approaches to Nurturing Children's Spirituality* (Eugene: Wipf and Stock, 2011), 108.

Stories also teach essential life skills. At one point in my life as a teacher, I told the story of King David and Bathsheba as part of a class study of Psalm 51.

"Psalm 51," I explained to my eight-year-old students, "was an example of how this powerful king said he was sorry, and what he wanted to do to make things better. Perhaps his example in psalm writing could help us when we needed to make amends for poor choices."

As we studied the narrative progression of Psalm 51 and observed its transition toward proclaiming God's praise, a child who had written more than his share of "sorry" notes, exclaimed, "S-w-e-e-e-t psalm!"

In addition to providing ideas for his next note of apology, this particular repentance psalm helped him find his place within the big and long story of God's people, where even King David needed to learn to express regret. Like King David, he could also go on to better things, such as teaching transgressors God's ways (v. 13), opening his lips to declare God's praise (v. 15), and offering God his contrite heart (v. 17).

In this case, King David's testimony of repentance helped a young boy. No doubt the boy's parents' or grandparents' stories of how they got into and out of trouble as children would also be helpful. My grandchildren certainly remain eager to hear these kinds of stories. I hope that such tales will help them to gain the skills they need to confess and make amends for their poor choices.

Can we relinquish enough pride to share episodes that expose us as vulnerable, fallible children of God, who regularly need to repent, confess, and make amends? Doing so may keep our relationships honest and healthy enough to speak more freely of God's presence in our lives.

The stories we share across generations serve manifold purposes. The Sunday school class of ten- to twelve-year-olds that I taught in 2011 considers me one of the "old people" in church. During a lesson about the ascension of Jesus, I took them outside to simulate a European-style ascension parade around the perimeter of our church's property. From the edges of the lot, we read progressive verses of the ascension and looked into the sky.

While listening to Scripture, the class became fascinated by an old, no-longer-used entrance. I responded to their curiosity by sharing some basic congregational history with them, including the struggle about cutting down an earlier generation's favourite climbing tree to make space for a needed addition. This story fascinated them. They were enticed enough to climb some of the remaining trees—trees that some of the students had never really noticed before. This in turn provided a window to review the story of Zacchaeus, the tax collector who climbed into a tree so that he could spot Jesus in a crowd. It also gave me a chance to see and compliment the tree-climbing skills of a girl who hadn't quite accepted me as her teacher.

One student, a recent immigrant, wondered how old the trees were. He tried to imagine when each tree had been planted. I explained how to count growth rings on the stump of a felled pine. This led other students to compare the pine's diameter to that of other trees on the lot, to speculate on their ages, and to wonder if any of the trees had taken root before our aging house of worship had been built.

In this situation, the Bible story provided an opportunity to explore the church property. It allowed students to connect with the history of our congregation, something that only a few of them could have heard from their own families. It linked the stories of God's people then and now, named parts of our congregational story, and provided the opportunity for some delightful sharing across the generations.

Recognizing and naming God's presence in our lives may emerge as we seek to stay in healthy relationships with the younger members of our biological or faith family. Sena Friesen wrote an article about role reversals that sometimes occur in such relationships. She described her relationship with an older college professor with whom she stayed in touch, and whose sage career advice she cherished. During one particular meeting, after providing some good solicited advice for her, he leaned forward and asked for hers.

"You're a daughter," he began. "I have a daughter about your age—a little younger . . . She's decided to go work in Afghanistan . . . My wife and I . . . she's our little girl! How can we . . ." He trails off.[6]

Sena reflected upon her own experience of wanting and needing to do something risky, and how she would have responded to advice from her parents. The conversation ended with her former professor thanking her for her wise advice. Because of this healthy intergenerational relationship, the sharing of wisdom, one of the attributes of God, flowed both ways.

My husband's family heritage includes stories of dislocation, capture, and starting life over in a new country. Of these ancestors, one great uncle remains. He has lived on three continents and tells great stories. Though his English remains flawed, my

---

6. Sena Friesen, "Role Reversal," *Purpose: Stories of Faith and Promise*, January 2011, 4.

older granddaughters love hearing tales of his many adventures. Since my in-laws and his wife have died, we include Onkel Hans at our larger family gatherings. His recent stories include examples of amazing forgiveness, and the charity of women from his hometown in Ukraine toward individuals who collaborated in the arrest and death of most of the town's men. These accounts are helping several generations claim God's presence in their heritage, and they are becoming a treasured part of our identity. They are a testimony to God's work in their lives, and in Onkel Hans's life as he matures spiritually and works at reconciling the suffering and injustice that he has experienced.

When we recognise the presence of God as we let go, name God's presence, and take hold of it, we can shape our experiences into stories. By integrating them with other stories that relay childhood pranks and "stars on the ceiling"—like the tale David Csinos fondly remembers his mother telling—we shape the family identity as a people who live in relationship with God.

Incorporating heritage stories into family traditions develops a safe space and opportunity for children to share their own anecdotes, including their personal experiences with God. Once children have been introduced to a space where speaking about religious experiences is respected, many will enter the conversation and surprise adults with their insights and spirituality. While we need to discern how much we share with children, they do have pastoral gifts and child wisdom to offer as a blessing to the wider family and faith community.

Holly Catterton Allen, director of the children and family ministry program at John Brown University, was inspired by what she learned about children through her participation in a small-groups-based church for several years. In the intimate, inter-generational setting where she worshiped, children regularly heard their parents pray and saw them minister to others in the group. Holly was amazed at the way children engaged in intercessory prayer and pastoral concern for their peers, as well as for the adults in the group.

Meetings often began with an "icebreaker" question. When one meeting opened with the question, "What are you afraid of?", a variety of responses were given.

"Gaining too much weight in my pregnancy."

"That I will die young like my dad."

"That I won't pass fourth grade."

"That Ben won't get his parole."

Finally, in a shaky voice, a young boy shared his fear: "I'm afraid to go to sleep because I have nightmares."

At this point, adults and another child in the group prayed for him. They shared how they had dealt with the same issue in their own lives and gave him the words of Psalm 4:8, 'I go to bed and sleep in peace. Lord, you keep me safe.'[7]

Sharing in children's experiences—whether difficult, as in the illustration above, or exhilarating—provides opportunities to connect them with God's big story. In the illustration, the child found a connection with the psalmist who also knew about the trial of sleeping in peace. Because we've been around longer, we have had the chance to familiarize

7. Holly Catterton Allen, "Nurturing children's Spirituality in Intergenerational Christian Settings," in *Children's Spirituality: Christian Perspectives, Research, and Applications*, ed. Donald Ratcliff (Eugene: Cascade Books, 2004), 226–28.

ourselves with the stories of God's people through the ages. When the time is right we can let younger people know that someone else has had similar experiences to theirs. We can share what happened to us, to our ancestors, or to biblical characters. This sharing can take place face to face, or in one of the electronic avenues we now use to communicate with our dear ones who are far and near.

In Chapter Two, I recommended reflecting on how God has been present in your life by drawing and annotating a "river-story" about your experiences. Such reflections could also become the basis for deep intergenerational sharing:

- As a church retreat activity, invite a willing senior to talk about his or her river-story. Invite younger participants to ask the story teller about particular events or experiences. This could lead to precious opportunities for deeper exchanges that might encourage others, young and old, to consider their own lives through their own river-stories.

- In a biological family setting, take the initiative on your birthday or anniversary to share the river-story of your life. Or at family gatherings, encourage others to reflect on events or relationships for which they are thankful, times they were frightened or embarrassed, felt really glad to be alive, and so on. My younger friend, David Csinos, shared his enthusiasm for a board game called *Reminisce* that helps families reflect upon and talk about their stories. He likes playing this game with his aunts and uncles because in the process, he learns so much about where he came from. These are a few ways of building storytelling cultures in which one can naturally integrate one's spirituality and awareness of the presence of God.

- When an event such as an older child's birthday approaches, invite the child to prepare his or her life or river-story to chart the past year and project what might lie ahead. Encourage other family members to reflect on ways they have seen God's gifts at work in and through that child.

Claiming Holidays as Holy Days

Our society may be moving beyond the time when the church year will influence our social calendar. For now, however, biological and spiritual families continue to gather around holidays that include Christmas, Easter, Thanksgiving, and perhaps All Saints' Day. Even summer vacations can be linked to the long season of Pentecost and its focus on the growth of the church.

These holidays provide marvellous opportunities for communicating faith and ideas across boundaries of age, whether we connect electronically or face-to-face. A careful look at the themes that reside in these events reveals many points of contact with the deep questions and needs that shape the lives of our family members. In addition, their underlying themes fit into the spiritual movements of letting go, naming God's presence, and taking hold of God's presence.

Christmas, Easter, and Pentecost each have a preparatory season. Whether it is Advent, Lent, or Pre-Pentecost—which is so under observed it doesn't even have its own name—the focus of these seasons is one of waiting and yearning.

Advent. This popular season connects with personal stories of longing for something more, perhaps rooted in dissatisfaction with current circumstances or dreams of a future grounded in hope. During Advent, look for activities that focus on letting go or learning to accept what we cannot change, and trusting God's timing:

- When Christmas gatherings occur during Advent, select stories from your memory bank that name and connect your expectations, longings, and dissatisfactions with Israel's longing for a Messiah and the gracious surprise of Emmanuel, God-with-us.
- Advent is also the season of planning, purchasing, and preparing gifts for grandchildren. As you do so, consider the messages your gifts bring. How do they relate to what is happening in each grandchild's life? Can the gift, or the message in the gift, reflect the way you see God at work in and through the recipient? What does the gift say about the giver? Does it connect to your hopes for your grandchild? Thoughtful gifts can do much to communicate love and values, whether or not the avenues for religious conversations are open.
- Set up a nativity scene with which your grandchildren can play. Act out the approach of Christmas, providing opportunities to tell the nativity story. If you live far away from your grandchildren, use Skype or other video teleconferencing options and ask them where to place things in your nativity scene as they watch you set it up.
- Consider giving your grandchildren sturdy nativity sets of their own to play with.

Compare the scenes that are set up in your home and theirs. Younger children may enjoy adding additional toy animals and other characters to the scene.

- Plan outings with a service component or help school age children learn about things that need mending in our world. As they learn and connect with the less fortunate, many Advent themes will become real for them.

- Challenge your grandchildren to memorize the Christmas story or an appropriate Christmas poem, and provide suitable incentives or coaching to make it an enjoyable activity. Coaching can happen in person or with the help of electronic communication.[8]

Lent. Similarly filled with longing and yearning for God's purposes to be accomplished, Lent is "laced with strange mixtures of excitement and fear, success and failure, loyalty and betrayal, affirmation and denial, life and death."[9] When the young people we love face such matters, we can name their struggles in our hearts or share them verbally as Lent or wilderness experiences. Whether the calendar is marked "Lent" or not, we find spiritual guidance by naming our struggles and identifying them with those of Jesus. It may even help us let go, to wait and trust God to work in the lives of our loved ones in the more challenging periods of their lives.

Lent presents wonderful opportunities to focus on living with Jesus. During Lent, invite your

---

8. For additional Advent ideas, see the free downloadable At-Home Advent booklets at www.mennonitechurch.ca/tiny/1418.

9. Olsen, *The Wisdom of the Seasons*, 62.

grandchildren to join you in activities that link thematically with Jesus' life:

- Plan a "wilderness" activity. Drive or hike into a nearby wildlife preserve or engage in something as simple as building a wilderness scene with toy animals on a blanket. Create hills to hide in by placing various sized boxes under the blanket. Talk about Jesus' time in the wilderness or encourage discussion about any wilderness experiences the young people you love are encountering.
- Jesus healed many people. Something as simple as cleaning and bandaging a cut provides the opportunity to identify with Jesus' healing ministry. Taking children along to visit people in the hospital or a personal care home builds that connection, too.
- Jesus was a great teacher and told many parables. With your grandchildren, create parables of your own. Or wonder together about some of Jesus' parables—like the sower and the seed in Matthew 13:1-23, or building a house on rock or on sand, in Matthew 7:24-27.
- Jesus had a prophetic ministry. He challenged the injustices of his day. Look for local or national injustices that are of interest to the young people you love. Find ways to involve them in making a prophetic statement, such as writing a letter or raising funds for an appropriate cause.
- Pancake Tuesday activities can introduce Lent effectively for people of all ages. Pour pancake batter onto the griddle in the shape of a young child's first initial. Share the origin

of Pancake Tuesday with older children. Perhaps they will choose to experience getting rid of rich foods for a season to focus on following Jesus.

- Ash Wednesday and Good Friday offer opportunities to think and talk about death together. Storybooks that treat this topic sensitively are easy to find in local libraries and bookstores.[10]

Pre-Pentecost. Falling between the ascension of Christ and the coming of the Holy Spirit for the birth of the church, Pre-Pentecost is a season of awaiting direction. Children and grandchildren often wonder where their lives are going and long for empowerment. Help them to identify with the disciples who waited and prayed before they were empowered to be the church and experienced new growth:

- Pre-Pentecost falls in the months of April and May. For those who live in the northern states or Canada, it often coincides with planting gardens and waiting for tender shoots to appear. Plant a garden with your grandchildren to experience rich opportunities for conversations about waiting for new growth—in the garden and in life.
- This season could launch the first camping or cottage excursion of the year and a relaxed

---

10. For additional activities and Lent rituals for Ash Wednesday, Maundy Thursday, and Good Friday, download Lent booklets from www.mennonitechurch.ca/tiny/1435. While they are written for parents and their children, the Holy Week activities also provide guidance for answering the tough questions children ask as they encounter the hard mystery of the cross.

campfire gathering. What stories might you share around the fire? Consider tales of family or congregational experiences that allude to the longing and holy potential of Pre-Pentecost.

- Bless the waiting periods in each other's lives and encourage anticipation for movement of the Holy Spirit among you. Share stories about how you have been blessed through the waiting periods in your life, and affirm your grandchildren for the good signs of patience and trust they are developing. By doing so, you encourage and bless their growth in these areas, and help them to accept waiting periods as difficult but good experiences. Learning to sing a favourite song or recalling a set of statistics from a favourite sport can teach patience when waiting is required.

Christmas, Easter, Pentecost, Thanksgiving, and All Saints' Day are the major holy days we observe in North America. The focus of these seasons is one of celebrating and naming God's presence.

Christmas. It is easy to celebrate a loving and giving God who came to be with us in human form at Christmas. We often forget that Jesus' birth happened in a complex and stressful period in a land that continues to groan for peace and justice. Jesus' mother experienced God's presence and connected with her spiritual ancestor, Hannah. She celebrated God her Savior with words from Hannah's song, "God's mercy is for those who fear him from generation to generation" (Luke 1:50).

In addition to Mary's famous song, The Magnificat, the Christmas narrative includes Zachariah's song,

The Benedictus, and the songs of angels glorifying God in heaven, "in excelsis Deo." No wonder we sing carols at Christmas! However, even if we don't sing or enjoy carols—and not all families do—Christmas gatherings are times to celebrate our loving and giving God by naming the wonders in our own lives.[11]

There are a number of ways to celebrate Christmas with grandchildren:

- Celebrate the beauty of the created order around you. Talk about your favourite places and what gives you a feeling of wonder about them.
- If there is a new baby to celebrate, wonder at his or her birth with older siblings. Retell the story of the child's arrival.
- Invite your grandchildren to join you in creating a list of the wonders in your lives. Thank God for these blessings before or after you open Christmas gifts together.
- Listen to or make music that helps you celebrate Christmas.
- In response to Mary's song of praise, the Magnificat, recall and share stories of how people you know have helped to make friends with rich and poor people.
- Recite or read the Christmas story from Luke 2:1-20 together.
- Add a special Jesus stocking to your other Christmas decorations. Invite family members to pick a charity and use the Jesus stocking to collect their donations.

11. Olsen, *The Wisdom of the Seasons*, 71.

Easter. We name the presence of God by the way we celebrate Easter and the resurrection of our suffering and victorious Servant Lord. Charles Olsen writes; "In Jesus, the God of Easter resides with us, knowing and participating in our everyday life of trial, loss, conflict, and testing—yet prevailing."[12] Easter is a time of joy, of vindication for doing the right thing, even when it is difficult. It is a time of new life and forgiveness, of second chances and glad reunions, and of engaging the mystery of life beyond death.

Easter also offers stories about surprising encounters with Christ. Such events leave the followers of Jesus in states of confusion and amazement. Their hearts burn within them (Luke 24:32), and send them running back to tell others about their encounters. Easter is an opportune time to connect these themes with the lives of children and grandchildren:

- Tell stories about family experiences filled with disturbing, energizing, and revealing dynamics.
- Share Scripture which has suddenly come alive with new meaning for you. Easter is a good opportunity to share selected moments from your spiritual journey, and help your family to connect with the bigger story of God and God's people.
- Host an Easter egg hunt that includes plastic eggs with short story problems tucked inside. After the eggs are gathered, share the stories in a group and decide on what the right but hard solution to the problem could be.
- Celebrate new understandings. Are there ideas or concepts that are new and exciting

---

12. Ibid., 72.

to your grandchildren? Ask about them and celebrate their growth in understanding. Link it to the new understandings of the disciples, if appropriate.

- Celebrate stories of forgiveness. Are there experiences of forgiveness in your family that can be gratefully remembered and celebrated? Is this an occasion to invite forgiveness, or to extend it for pain that has been inflicted? Whether or not you link this verbally, to God's great forgiving acts through Jesus life, death, and resurrection, extending forgiveness will help you identify with your crucified and resurrected Lord.

Pentecost. As Christmas celebrates God's coming to be with us in human form, Pentecost celebrates the coming of God's spirit to empower us from within. This is a festival of taking hold, of empowered response. Not only does the gift of God's Spirit make the presence of Christ real to us, it also enables us to dream and implement new visions of participating in God's ongoing work. Together we lean toward the day when heaven will be on earth; God's home will be among mortals, God will wipe away every tear from their eyes, and death will be no more (Revelation 21:1-4).

Pentecost ushers in the church season called ordinary time. It connects our ordinary lives to the empowerment of God's Spirit, which is at work in the church and in the world. At Pentecost, the Holy Spirit breathed new life into the disciples and gave birth to the church. Lectionary texts for this season feature the work of the church. The themes of Pentecost can be celebrated in a number of ways:

- Celebrate the completion of projects and the launching of new ones. School age grandchildren will be completing their school year, so completed projects should be easy to find.
- Celebrate family life experiences where good communication broke the silence and re-established floundering relationships.
- Celebrate gifts of spiritual discernment, of endurance, and of hanging in there with each other as a family or church community, despite differences.[13]
- Find other points of contact between this season and ordinary life, and use them as opportunities to build connections between personal stories and the bigger stories of God's people.
- Hold a birthday-of-the-church party with grandchildren to share the story of Pentecost. Select stories from congregational history to share with them as well.
- The Holy Spirit came with a great wind. Choose a way to play with the wind such as flying a kite or playing with pinwheels. Draw connections between wind and the breath inside our bodies, which is another of God's great gifts to us.

Thanksgiving. Both Canada and the U.S. celebrate the feast of thanksgiving, although at different times of the year. In Canada, it originated as a thankful celebration of the gifts of harvest. In the U.S., it was first celebrated to thank God for helping settlers survive a tough winter. While Thanksgiving hasn't been built into the liturgical calendar as deliberately

13. Ibid., 74.

as Advent, Christmas, Lent, Easter, and Pentecost, it is a festival that is growing in importance for Christians who live on an increasingly endangered planet.

I once attended an Aboriginal teaching session about creation care, led by the Cree theologian and former moderator of the United Church of Canada, Reverend Stan McKay. He taught that dangers exist for Mother Earth when we misunderstand what it means for humanity to *have dominion* over creation (Genesis 1:26). Having dominion does not mean to "rule over," or to use to our immediate advantage, but to "steward" or "care for."

In the Bible, God offered humans a sacred balance at the dawn of creation, but Adam and Eve made choices in the Garden of Eden that upset the balance. Instead of noting those poor choices—and the fall of humans—the story of our beginnings is often referred to as "the fall of creation."

Celebrating Thanksgiving with our families provides precious opportunities to relearn the important disciplines of respect, thanksgiving, and harmonious interdependence with the land. God has placed us here as caretakers and cocreators. We ignore these truths at the earth's peril. While we can nurture attitudes of gratitude and a healthy connection with the food we eat all year, Thanksgiving celebrations have a formational potential.

Small actions help us to reclaim our place in the sacred balance of land, water, and the rest of creation, when we celebrate thanksgiving with children and grandchildren:

- Use thanksgiving feasts to celebrate the journey from the farm to your forks, as well as from seed to fruit. If you have access to land, grow produce or raise small animals as an intergenerational project with food to be shared on Thanksgiving.

- If you don't have access to land, sensitivity to food issues and the miracles of plant growth are easily developed by growing a windowsill herb garden—a great activity to do together with grandchildren.
- If growing your own food isn't possible, shop at local markets or challenge older grandchildren to research the farm to fork journeys of the foods on your Thanksgiving table.
- Look on the internet for classic indigenous prayers of gratitude. They give thanks to the different aspects of creation and inspire appreciation. Use one of these prayers to stimulate a list of things in creation for which you are grateful.
- Along with your invitation to a Thanksgiving celebration, ask children and grandchildren to think of family experiences in creation for which they are grateful. Take some time at the Thanksgiving table to share words of appreciation for the many ways you bless each other.
- Make your family Thanksgiving an experience of taking hold of God's presence, of responding to God's call to remember that the earth is the Lord's. Choose some of the above activities, and read Psalm 104 at the beginning or end of the meal.

All Saints' Day. This church holiday receives less attention than those preceding it. Perhaps this is because it is overshadowed by Halloween, its secularized and controversial precursor.

Although Halloween was not officially recognized or celebrated at Winnipeg Mennonite Elementary School where I taught, the students were very well aware of it. Many children went trick-or-treating. Knowing how to best acknowledge this reality was challenging. I encouraged children to journal about their experiences, and focused on Halloween's Christian meaning as All Hallows' Eve, the evening before All Saints' Day, in our class devotions. On the morning after Halloween, I introduced an All Saints' Day prayer frame to help us recall how we are blessed by the memories of people and pets that had died.

A prayer frame provides the beginning and the end of the prayer and allows individuals to insert their comments within that structure. Students participated actively in the preparatory conversation for this activity, and many important memories of loved ones surfaced. The following prayer, in which the frame is bolded, reflects on the grandfather Alexandra never got to meet. It became her favourite prayer of the year.

> **On All Saints' Day we remember**
> I remember when my dad told me a story about his dad that he hardly got to see his dad he only got to see him till he was six.
> And he died when my dad was in grade one.
> **Their memories still bless us.**

Halloween and All Saints' Day provide unique opportunities for reflecting on the end of life and celebrating the legacy of those who have died. Perhaps your congregation does not celebrate All Saints' Day at all, and instead celebrates Eternity Sunday, or Memorial Sunday, on the last Sabbath before Advent. While it isn't tied to the excitement of Halloween, it provides similar opportunities to encourage reflection.

In my congregation, we have an extended candle lighting service on this Sunday, where many come forward to light candles in memory of loved ones that have died. Most will share the names of their loved ones with the congregation, and some will share a descriptive phrase or anecdote of remembrance. In recent years, the stream of candle lighters has grown to include people of all ages. Some invite their extended families to join them for this significant ritual and then go out for a family lunch afterwards, so memory sharing can continue and flow more freely. When those who died more recently have lived and died well, the blessing of their lives continues. Their legacy is fostered.

If you cannot participate in such a congregational service with your grandchildren, there are other ways to get together and adapt some of those activities:

- Invite thoughts about pets and family members who have died. Use the prayer frame above to develop a short ritual.
- Light candles for those who have died, name those loved ones, and state the ways in which their memories are still a blessing.
- Tell stories of family members who died a long time ago.
- Start or add onto a family tree, and tell anecdotes about places your ancestors lived or adventures they might have faced.
- Tell stories about some of the founding members of your church tradition.

Conclusion

What a variety of stories and celebrations we have to claim as tools for building strong relationships with our biological and spiritual grandchildren! Allow this chapter's focus on stories and holidays to encourage your natural drive toward storytelling.

Good storytelling is as important for the younger generation's need to grow roots as it is for the senior generation's need to leave legacies. If we grow together in awareness of our place in God's big story and God's family through the ages, we find greater meaning and hope in our identities. What better security can we offer the young as they live into a rapidly changing future?

While a storytelling culture shapes our identity as people of God, celebrating holy days creates a resilient framework for us to live out our lives as God's people, whether we are young, old, or in between. By embracing the underlying themes and questions of these church year events, we build our ability to cope with life's many joys, fears, and sorrows.

Share stories whenever you have the opportunity. Choose the holy days that best fit your family's realities, and gradually add new and meaningful traditions to your celebrations. When one new tradition becomes a natural part of your life rhythm, add another.

As you celebrate your place within God's big story and practice the art of spiritual grandparenting, may your relationships with each other and with God grow in depth and character.

Reflection and Discussion Questions

Sharing our stories as testimony

1. Reflect on a storyteller whose stories attracted you. Which aspects of his or her storytelling style added to the story's appeal?
2. What role does storytelling play in the way you relate to the young people who are dear to you? Share with each other life shaping stories that come to mind.
3. What intergenerational opportunities for sharing stories do you enjoy, or could you promote in your family or congregation?
4. What stories in your life parallel stories from the annals of God's people in the Bible and church history?
5. What are the difficulties and benefits of naming God's presence in our stories?

Preparatory holy days: Advent, Lent, and Pre-Pentecost

1. What traditions can you draw on to connect with these seasons' themes of waiting and preparation? Share these traditions with each other.
2. What stories from the Bible, church history, current literature, or movie lore reflect these themes of waiting and preparation? How could these stories help you engage these seasons more deeply?
3. How do the lives of the young people who are dear to you connect with themes of waiting and yearning? What holy discontent propels them forward to God's intentions for their lives?

Celebratory holy days: Christmas, Easter, Pentecost, Thanksgiving, and All Saints' Day

1. What church holiday celebrations do you share with the young people who are dear to you?
2. How do the themes of these celebrations connect with your life experiences?
3. What other celebrations provide opportunities for naming and proclaiming the wonders in our lives, vindication for doing the right but hard thing, the empowerment of knowing God is with us, and of learning to live in respect, thanksgiving, and interdependence?

Epilogue

So how can we, who are in the last third of life, pass the faith to young people who are in the first third of their lives, whether or not they have chosen to follow Christ? This book named some of the major challenges we face on this quest and briefly addressed them. Together we have considered how society and culture have impacted this role; how to recognize, tend, and learn to share our own spirituality; to understand how faith grows in the young and the older; what to do if our beloved children or grandchildren reject our faith; and how to connect our stories to God's big story.

We do not undertake our spiritual journeys in isolation. We belong to the long, wide movement of God's children through time and place. Claiming our place within God's story roots us in our God-given identity. We grow to know who we are and *whose* we are. What a gift for young people who need also need to know who they are, whose they are, and where they are headed!

How the Holy Spirit moves in the lives of our beloved young people is a mystery that we cannot, and need not, control. Instead, we serve as midwives to the process by loving, accepting, and encouraging them along the way. As non-threatening conversation partners, we provide safe spaces for our loved ones to air doubts and raise questions. Their doubts and questions won't threaten our own faith if we trust that God will lead them through their struggles, just as God leads us through ours. And along the way, we may learn a few things. Who knows how God may surprise and teach us through the young?

No matter how unfamiliar their choices and life directions may seem to us, we can pray for our young people and entrust them to God's merciful guidance. When opportunities are right and the Spirit nudges us to do so, we can pray *with* them. Prayers of blessing and intercession are powerful tools to align others with God's hopes and dreams for them. They are even more precious to God than they are to us. Blessing connects us all, wherever we are on our life and faith journeys, because blessing emerges from God's graciousness.

May the words of this book encourage you in the art of spiritual grandparenting and equip you to pass your faith on to the younger people who are dear to you.

A Prayer for Faithful Generations

We are Christian Seniors who love the young;
may God bless our relating, speaking, and
listening,
so that our words, thoughts and actions bless
our grandchildren and the church's children.

May we and those we love be sheltered and
nourished
by the deep awareness
that we are all part of God's big story;
that we are loved, treasured, and gifted
by God the Father, the Son, and the Holy Spirit.

May God's love and truth be ever
in our hearts and minds
to help us walk in God's ways
and know God's peace,
healing, and hope,
so that God's blessings can keep flowing
through us to our grandchildren and others
as long as God grants us life.
Amen.

The Author

Elsie H. R. Rempel is a young senior, a "baby boomer," and an experienced member of "club sandwich" generation. She is the devoted grandmother of four children ages one to twelve. A trained teacher with many years of experience in Christian school classrooms, Elsie devoted much of the last decade to  Mennonite Church Canada faith formation ministries. During that time, she gathered, developed, and shared faith forming resources for people of all ages. She also obtained her MA in theology. Her theses, "Mennonites, Children, and Communion," reveals just one of the ways she is working to integrate children more deeply into the life of the church.

Most recently, Elsie wrote curriculum for vacation Bible school, edited a Bible study series on Revelation, and served as a mentor to elementary school teachers in Zambia's Southern Province through a Mennonite Central Committee program. Currently she seeks to encourage and mentor church lay leaders of all ages through her ministry as Mennonite Church Canada formation consultant.

Elsie belongs to Charleswood Mennonite Church in Winnipeg, Manitoba. She and her husband, Peter Rempel, have three married adult children, all of whom live near the Rempel home in Winnipeg.

CPSIA information can be obtained at www.ICGtesting.com
Printed in the USA
BVOW010233080612

292072BV00004B/2/P